Nate Saint

Operation Auca

Nate Saint

Operation Auca

Nancy Drummond

CF4·K

10 9 8 7 6 5 4 3 2 1

© Copyright 2012 Nancy Drummond

paperback ISBN: 978-1-84550-979-8

epub ISBN: 978-1-78191-083-2

mobi: ISBN: 978-1-78191-084-9

Published by
Christian Focus Publications,
Geanies House, Fearn, Ross-shire,
IV20 1TW, Scotland, UK.
www.christianfocus.com
e-mail: info@christianfocus.com

Cover design by Daniel van Straaten
Cover illustration Pino Avonto
Illustrations by Jeff Anderson
Printed and bound by Nørhaven, Denmark

Contents

An Eye-Opening Experience

Nate Saint peered eagerly over the edge of his big brother Sam's Challenger biplane. His heart thumped against his ribs in anticipation of takeoff.

"You ready for this, Thanny?" Sam asked, affectionately using his little brother's nickname. Nate nodded enthusiastically. "Well then, off we go!"

Sam adjusted his goggles and glanced back to be sure Nate was strapped securely in place in the open cockpit. Nate grinned, and Sam grinned back. Then the engine sputtered and roared to life. They were on their way.

The year was 1930, and Nate was only seven years old. But as he felt the jolt of takeoff in the pit of his stomach and watched the airstrip drop away beneath him, he knew exactly what he wanted from life. This was his first flight, but it certainly wouldn't be his last. Nate was destined and determined to spend his life around airplanes.

Sam waved his arm toward the landscape below. "Take a look, Thanny. Anything look familiar?"

As Sam banked the biplane and flew over their town of Huntingdon, Pennsylvania, Nate could make out familiar landmarks. He saw the Presbyterian Church where his family attended services every Sunday and Wednesday. He saw the schoolhouse where his friends would be amazed to hear about his latest adventure. Then Sam turned the plane slightly and pointed down. There was the Saint house, with his father's workshop and the giant wooden roller coaster in the back yard. Nate smiled. Even from the air, his house looked like a great place to live.

"Wow," was all Nate could manage to say.

Nate's house was anything but ordinary. His parents, Lawrence and Katherine Saint, loved their children and believed they should be free to dream big dreams and try to achieve them. Lawrence was an artist, and Katherine was the daughter of an inventor. When their children came up with wild schemes— such as sleeping on the roof or building a huge model railroad—Lawrence and Katherine rarely said no. Instead, they would help make their children's dreams and schemes a reality. With a working roller coaster, beds on the roof, and another interesting project always in the works, the Saint household was an exciting place to be.

While traditional rules like mealtime and bedtime were rarely observed, following God's laws was a big deal in the Saint household. Sundays were always regarded as the Lord's Day. The family woke early and had breakfast together. Then they attended Sunday School and church services. After church, they ate lunch together and had a time of family prayer and

Bible study. They also went to Sunday night services and Wednesday evening Bible study as a family.

During the rest of the week, when he wasn't riding the roller coaster, sleeping on the roof, or swinging from the giant tree swing, Nate loved to build models of all sorts of things. With his brothers, Ben and Phil, Nate built a huge, working model railroad. By himself, Nate built a six-foot-long glider that really flew. He usually didn't have directions or kits for building what he made; he just looked at pictures of what he wanted to build, and somehow he knew exactly what to do.

In addition to building things, Nate was always inventing. He liked to take old things and make them new again. He liked to find things that worked well and make them work even better. He also liked to come up with brand new ideas and find ways to make them work. Nate's inventions were so good and useful, some of them won awards at local hobby shows before he turned ten years old.

As the plane descended and taxied to a stop that day in 1930, Nate was in love with flying. He lingered in the cockpit, reverently touching the controls and examining the gauges. Sam climbed from the plane and leaned on the edge of the open cockpit.

"What do you say, Thanny? You like it?"

Nate nodded. "It's the greatest feeling in the world!"

"I agree," Sam said, lifting Nate from the cockpit and ruffling his hair affectionately. "Now, let's go get some dinner. I do believe I could smell Mama's gravy from a thousand feet up."

Nate grinned. With one last longing look at the biplane, he followed his brother. But in his heart he said a little prayer that it wouldn't be long before he would be flying again. In just a few years, Nate's dream came true.

When Nate was ten, he took his second airplane ride with Sam. Sam's new plane was a 1933 Stinson with an enclosed cockpit. Even better, in this new type of plane, the pilot and co-pilot or passenger sat side by side.

"I've been reading about flying," Nate told Sam.

Sam grinned at him. "Got the flying bug, have you? Well, today we might just see how much you've learned from those books of yours."

As Sam prepared for takeoff, Nate watched him closely. They taxied down the runway and climbed into the sky. Nate checked every gauge and observed every needle. He drank in every move Sam made, making mental notes of proper procedures and comparing his mental notes to what he had read.

Sam noticed Nate's attention to detail and obvious love of flying. He remembered feeling that way himself, many years ago. When the plane was high above the green grid of farms and pastures, Sam turned to Nate with a smile.

"Okay, little brother. Let's see what you can do," Sam said.

"What?"

"Take the controls, Thanny. Let's see if you've learned anything from all your studying."

"Really?" Nate was thrilled and terrified, all at once. "I have the controls?"

"She's all yours," Sam said, lacing his fingers behind his head and leaning back.

Nate could hardly believe it. He stretched his feet to reach the pedals and gripped the control wheel. When he pulled back gently on the wheel, the little plane climbed toward the clouds. When he pushed forward, the nose dipped toward the landscape below. Nate's whole body tingled with excitement and he laughed out loud. He was flying! But Nate Saint's journey was only beginning.

"This is the best day of my life," Nate told Sam as he made the plane dip and turn. "I want to fly forever and ever and ever!"

"I'm glad you're enjoying yourself," Sam said with a chuckle. "But I don't think the fuel will last forever and ever and ever. Or didn't you read about fuel gauges in those books of yours?"

"You know what I mean," Nate protested, laughing.

"Yes," Sam said. "I know exactly what you mean."

From that day on, flying and airplanes were Nate's first love. He read about planes, talked about planes, built model planes, and dreamed about planes. Nate knew God had a plan for his life, and he was sure flying would be part of that plan. He could hardly wait to ride in a plane again and maybe even to take the controls. And someday, he hoped he would have a chance to fly a plane of his very own.

Finding God's Path

On a warm summer night when Nate was thirteen, his life changed forever. He was at camp in the Pocono Mountains, having a wonderful time. On Saturday night, the campers crowded around a bonfire and listened to a counselor talk about Jesus and how he died to forgive the sins of every person who trusts in him. The counselor said Jesus chose to lay down his perfect life so believers could someday live in heaven with him.

Nate had heard the story a hundred times, but that night it meant something new and exciting to him. The counselor asked if anyone would like to pray and ask Jesus to forgive their sins and be the Lord of their life. Nate raised his hand. He had always believed in God, but he had never personally invited Jesus to be in charge of his life.

With the bonfire flickering before him, Nate bowed his head. "God, I'm so sorry I'm a sinner," he prayed. "Please forgive me for my sins. Thank you for dying to pay the price for my sins. I want to live my life for you. Please come into my heart and be the Lord of my life."

When Nate lifted his head, he felt different. He knew that his life was different than it had ever been before. That night, Nate began a new, personal walk with God.

Only a few months later, Nate's new faith faced a challenge. In the spring of 1937, just after Nate turned fourteen, he woke one morning with a sharp pain in his right leg.

"Mom," Nate called weakly.

His mother rushed into his room. "What is it, Nate?"

"My leg hurts so bad," Nate told her. "It hurts way down in my bone. It just throbs and aches. And I feel all hot and sweaty."

Katherine Saint felt her son's forehead. "My goodness," she exclaimed. "You're burning up with fever! I'm calling the doctor."

The family doctor came and examined Nate. He spent a long time examining a cut on Nate's leg. Finally, he stood, shaking his head solemnly.

"When did you get this cut, son?" the doctor asked.

"Several weeks ago, when we were sledding," Nate answered. "But, doc, it isn't the cut that hurts. It's down in my bones."

"Well," the doctor said, "it seems you've developed a bone infection called osteomyelitis from that small cut. There's really nothing we can do but hope for the best."

For weeks, Nate's right leg was swollen and painful, and he burned with fever. The doctor came to see Nate often, but at that time there were no drugs to treat osteomyelitis. Antibiotics were still several years from being developed. The doctor and Nate's family simply had to pray that Nate's body was strong enough to fight the infection.

During his illness, Nate slept a lot. When he was awake, he took some time to get to know God better. Nate's sister, Rachel, read him Bible stories and tales of famous missionaries like David Livingstone. His father often came to pray with him. But there were also many quiet moments when Nate was alone. In these moments, he studied his Bible and prayed.

"God," Nate prayed, "I know you say everything we go through is for a reason. I don't know what your reason is for this infection, but I really want to do more with my life. I want you to do something in my life to bring you glory. Whether I live or die, I want my future to be completely yours."

Nate knew the infection he had could kill him. He wasn't afraid to die because he knew God had promised him a home in heaven. But even though he wasn't afraid to die, Nate wanted to live. He wanted to fly again, and he wanted to do something great for God. That was why Nate prayed and promised God that if he was healed from the osteomyelitis, he would give God his whole life. God could use Nate to do his will.

After several weeks of illness, Nate's infection began to go away. Even though Nate could not walk on his infected leg yet, he began to feel better and move around the house, crawling on his hands and knees. He drew up plans for a new sailboat and made new model planes from scraps of paper. He was so glad to be out of bed, doing things he loved. But even in his busyness, Nate didn't forget the promise he made to God.

When he was fully recovered, Nate began teaching Sunday School at the Baptist church his family then attended. He also became president of his local Baptist Young People's Union, and he remained faithful in his prayer and Bible study. Nate didn't want to lose the closeness he had developed with God during his illness. He wanted to figure out God's plan for his life.

In addition to keeping his commitment to God, Nate also had a lot of schoolwork to make up. He had been out of school for months because of his infection, leaving him far behind his classmates. Sometimes it seemed he would never finish the mountain of work he faced, but Nate was determined, and he finished every assignment.

As he grew older, Nate found he was easily bored with regular classroom learning. He tried going to school during the day and working a job at night, but that wasn't for him. Then he tried working during the day and going to school at night in Philadelphia. That was better. Nate graduated from high school in 1941.

When Nate graduated, there was a war—World War II—going on in Europe and Asia. Although

America was not yet involved, the whole world seemed restless, and Nate was restless, too. He worked as a welder and tree trimmer. He pumped gas and did odd jobs. Nothing made him happy, however. He knew God had put a love of flying in his heart, but that kind of job seemed out of reach for a young man with no money and no experience. Nate wasn't sure what to do or where to go.

For a change of scenery, Nate volunteered to deliver a new truck to a missionary family in Virginia. He enjoyed the trip and the thrill of seeing new things and new places. Once the truck was delivered, however, Nate realized he had no money and no way to get home to Pennsylvania. He tried hitchhiking, but cars were scarce on the back roads of Virginia. Then he saw a train passing by in the distance, and he had a seemingly brilliant idea: He could jump on and hitch a ride in an empty boxcar.

Nate made the jump successfully and found himself in a rickety boxcar with several hobos who were also hitching a ride.

One of the hobos offered Nate a toothless grin. "Welcome aboard, friend," he said.

"Thanks," Nate said, settling himself on the uneven floor of the boxcar. It was hard to get comfortable, but at least he was moving again. He would be home before he knew it.

Nate dozed through a half dozen stops as the train rolled northward. But in one town, heavy hands pounded on the side of the boxcar, and the door slid open, flooding the narrow space with light.

"Get up, you ruffians," a gruff police officer ordered.

Nate scrambled to his feet. The officer sidled up to him. Nate swallowed hard, fighting the cottony lump that had risen in his throat.

"You don't look like a hobo," the officer said.

"No, sir," Nate answered.

"No, sir, you don't look like one? Or no, sir, you ain't one?" the officer asked.

"I'm not a hobo, sir."

"Well, we'll see what the judge has to say about that," the officer said. "Now come along to the jail."

"Jail!" Nate was shocked. "But what did I do?"

The officer chuckled. "Jumping a train is illegal. Or didn't you know that either?"

Nate followed miserably behind the officer. He really had not known it was illegal to hitch a ride on a train. He felt ashamed and angry and frustrated and frightened, all at once.

After a long night in a chilly jail cell, Nate and the hobos were brought before a judge. The judge peered at them, evaluating each man carefully. He sentenced the hobos to jail for jumping a train. But when he got to Nate, he paused.

"Son, you don't look like a hobo," the judge said.

"No, your honor," Nate said. "I was just trying to get home."

The judge tipped his head slightly. "I see. Well, since this is a first offense, and you seem truly sorry, I will offer you two punishment options."

"Thank you, your honor," Nate said.

"First, you may serve ten days in jail," the judge said. "Or, if you'd rather, you may pay a ten-dollar fine and be on your way. Which will it be, son?"

The judge expected Nate to pay the fine, but Nate had no money.

"I'll take the ten days in jail, your honor," Nate said.

The judge raised his eyebrows. "Well, then, I sentence you to ten days in jail. And son?"

"Yes, your honor?"

"No more jumping trains. I don't want to see you in my courtroom again."

Nate shook his head quickly. "You won't see me again, your honor. Thank you, your honor."

So, Nate spent ten days in jail. When he was released, Nate hitchhiked back to Pennsylvania as fast as he could, vowing never to go to jail again. And he never did.

Eventually, Nate got a job as a general hand at the Flying Dutchman Air Service just outside Philadelphia. It was a dream job. Nate was around planes every day. He could see the powerful wings, touch the smooth fuselage, smell the fumes of fuel, and hear the roar and rumble of engines. He learned what made airplanes work—inside and out. He began to feel the pieces of his life were finally coming together.

While working for the Flying Dutchman Air Service, Nate took his first official flying lesson. It was everything he dreamed it would be. Soaring through the sky, high above the cares of the world, Nate was flooded with pure joy. He knew it was where he belonged. From that moment on, Nate saved every penny he could. He soon had enough to buy a small airplane of his own. Nate flew every time he had the opportunity, logging many flight hours and soon earning his private pilot's license.

Sam, Nate's older brother, had become a pilot for American Airlines. He saw Nate's accomplishments and wanted to help him achieve his dreams. One day Sam came to see Nate. Sam sat on Nate's bed while Nate stretched out and read a book.

"How would you like a new job?" Sam asked Nate.

"Doing what?" Nate barely looked up from his flight manual.

"Well," Sam said, "I heard we might just have an apprentice airline mechanic position available for American Airlines."

Nate's book fell closed and he sat up abruptly. "Do you mean it?"

"Sure do, Thanny," Sam insisted with a grin. "How soon can you get yourself to LaGuardia Field in New York City?"

"Are you kidding?" Nate said, letting out a whoop of joy that brought his mother running. "I can be there yesterday!"

Nate was overjoyed! He had a great new job in a great new city doing something he loved. Despite the turmoil in the world, Nate felt great peace in his life. Unfortunately, his sense of peace wouldn't last long.

The World War Detour

On December 7, 1941, Japan attacked Pearl Harbor in Hawaii. The worldwide turmoil had finally come to America. Many young men—some with jobs and families—were drafted into military service to fight in World War II. Because Nate was employed as an airline mechanic, and the airline industry was considered an "essential industry", he was not drafted. But as the months of war dragged on and more and more people were asked to serve, Nate felt increasingly uncomfortable. He wanted to do his part.

Although Nate loved his job, in November 1942 he couldn't stand it any longer.

"Sam," he told his brother one afternoon, "I'm quitting."

"Quitting what?" Sam asked.

"My job. I'm going to enlist in the Army."

Sam's head snapped up. "But, Thanny," he protested, "we're in an essential industry. You don't need to enlist. Your skills are needed here at home."

Nate shook his head. "Airplane mechanics are a dime a dozen, Sam. You know that. And I don't have a family like you do. I should be out fighting for my country."

"I'm just saying it seems like a waste of your valuable skills, that's all," Sam said.

"Aw, don't be so disappointed. I plan to try for the Army Air Corps. That way all those skills you taught me will be put to good use. How does that sound?"

Sam smiled sadly. "I just worry about you, little brother. I'm proud that you want to fight for your country, but I hate to see you go."

Nate elbowed Sam playfully. "I guess God can protect me out there better than you can in here, right?"

Sam grinned. "You got me there. I can't argue with that one!"

Nate quit his job immediately and enlisted in the Army. Although his goal was to join the Army Air Corps, where he could use his flying skills, he was accepted instead as a regular soldier. Just before the end of 1942, Nate shipped out to Camp Luna in New Mexico. The days were long and the training was hard. Nate fell into bed each night weak with exhaustion, but he still prayed every night that God would open the door for him to work on planes and fly them again.

A few months into his training, Nate's prayers were answered. He was accepted into an Army school in Los Angeles where he would learn to work on C-47 cargo planes. After graduating from the program, Nate was sent to Missouri. In Missouri, he learned new things and gained valuable experience working on C-47s. He was glad to be working with planes again, but he still prayed for an opportunity to fly. Soon, those prayers were answered too. He was accepted into the Air Cadet Training Program in Iowa. He was going to fly again!

Nate was on his way to his fourth home in only six months, but this time the ride was thrilling because he was headed to the future of his dreams. As his train rolled past lush, green fields and wide-open farmland, Nate bowed his head.

"God," he silently prayed, "I can't express my thankfulness. You heard my prayers, and you're giving me what I always dreamed of. Thank you for being with me and guiding my steps. Thank you for making my dreams a reality. As this new chapter of my life begins, please help me to order my steps in your Word, God. Amen."

Through all the moving and changing in his life, Nate had never forgotten his faith. He went to church whenever he could and prayed and read his Bible daily. He was faithful to the promise he made to God five years earlier when he had osteomyelitis. God was directing Nate's path.

The first three months at Morningside College in Iowa were long and hard. Nate's daily routine included hours of classroom work on flying and airplanes, as well as fitness routines, chores, and drills. Sometimes there were special tasks, like night marches, that made the time seem even slower. Nate didn't always like it, but he pushed on and kept doing his best. He knew he had to make it through the tough part of his training if he ever wanted to fly an Army plane.

After the last night march of their training—only two days before they were scheduled to start flying—Nate noticed a familiar pain in his right leg. As he undressed for bed, he noticed puffy, red swelling around the old osteomyelitis scar. Nate knew what that meant. The osteomyelitis was back, and his flight training was over. The Army would not send someone with a recurring infection overseas, and they would not waste time and money training a pilot they could not send into combat. Nate let out a tiny moan of pure grief.

"Hey, Saint, you okay?" Nate's bunkmate asked.

Nate gulped down the lump of frustration that was swelling in his throat. "Yeah, sure. I'm fine. Why?"

His bunkmate rolled over and peered down from the top bunk. "I thought I heard you groaning down there. Boy, they sure did push us hard tonight, man. I can barely move!"

Nate looked down, trying to hide his troubled face. "It was brutal," he agreed. "But at least it's the last one."

"Isn't that the truth? And tomorrow we head out to the airfield. We can finally do what we came here to do!"

"Yeah," Nate agreed. *You'll head out to the airfield*, Nate thought, *but I'll be in the infirmary seeing the doctor.*

"Well, goodnight, Saint," his bunkmate said, rolling back onto the bunk. "Get some sleep. We're gonna need it when we become flyboys tomorrow."

Nate bid his bunkmate goodnight and buried his face in his pillow. Tears of disappointment burned Nate's eyes. He wondered why God let him get so close to his dream, only to have it taken away from him. The pain in his heart was so much worse than the pain in his leg. He wondered what future plans God could possibly have for someone like him.

The next morning, which was Nate's 20th birthday, he said goodbye to his fellow students. They all headed to the airfield while Nate headed to an Army hospital. The doctors confirmed what Nate already knew: the osteomyelitis was back. His Army records were changed to show Nate was physically fit only for ground duty and only in the United States, not overseas and not as a pilot. Nate's dream was over.

Nate was heartbroken, but he was still determined to be the best soldier he could be. He believed he should work hard wherever he was, and he still believed God had a plan for his life. When his osteomyelitis had healed again, Nate was shipped out to Texas, where he served as a barracks chief over fifty men. It was hard work, but through his leadership position, Nate was able to inspire and encourage many soldiers to renew their faith in God. Whatever position he was in, Nate lived his life in a way that pointed others to God.

Just before Christmas 1943, Nate learned he was being transferred to Indiana. There he would serve as a crew chief working on C-47 cargo planes. It renewed a glimmer of hope in Nate's heart. If he couldn't be flying, at least he could be around planes every day, hearing the thunder of the engines and knowing he was responsible for making each plane fly its best. Nate was also eager to go to Indiana because his brother, Phillip, an artist and evangelist, often spoke at a nearby conference center. After so much time away, Nate was hungry for direct contact with his close-knit family.

The first chance he got, Nate drove from his new base in Indiana out to the conference center. He found Phillip preparing sermons.

"Phil! It's so good to see you," Nate said.

"Let me look at you, Thanny," Phillip said. "My, my! You're all grown up now. Not the boy that left home, that's for sure. Wouldn't Mom be surprised?"

Nate thrilled at the chance to hear news from home. "Have you been back recently?" he asked. "How is everyone?"

"I was back a few weeks ago. Everyone is well. Mom still cooks for an army, even though there aren't many of us there. Dad is well. They both send their love. And, of course, Rachel is as bossy as ever!"

Nate laughed. "I think that's her mission as our big sister. I'm glad everyone is well. I can't wait to see them all again. Have you heard from Sam?"

"He and his family are well. The airline is keeping him busy, that's for sure," Phillip answered.

"And how are you, Phil? Do you like what you're doing?"

Phillip nodded. "I feel very blessed that God chose me to spread His gospel. And I get to use my artistic talents while I do it. It doesn't get any better than that. But I guess the happiest place for a man to be is right in the center of God's will for his life. Anyway, enough about me! I want to hear about all of your adventures."

Nate and Phillip talked for hours. Every time he was able, Nate slipped away to visit Phillip at the conference center. It was so good to be with family again, and Phillip encouraged Nate in his faith and his walk with the Lord. That made him a better man and a better soldier.

As Nate settled into his new routine in Indiana, he got to know the soldiers who worked with him. One soldier was just finishing his certification as an official airplane mechanic. He showed Nate how to get assistance from the Army for civilian training as a certified airplane mechanic. During his spare time, Nate studied hard and soon earned his certification. It seemed that God had once again opened a door for Nate to have airplanes in his life, even if it wasn't the way Nate had originally dreamed.

When he couldn't get to church, Nate often listened to sermons on the radio by a Detroit-based preacher named Dr. John Zoller. In late 1944, when Nate was sent to Detroit on a special project with the Ford Motor Company, he hoped to visit Dr. Zoller's church. He loved the way Dr. Zoller preached and explained God's Word, and he wanted to hear a message in person. On New Year's Eve, Nate got that opportunity.

As he walked into the church that night, Nate knew what he wanted from life. He wanted to fly planes and work on planes, and he wanted a comfortable home, maybe near his family, where he could someday raise a family of his own. But when Nate walked out of the church service a few hours later, his vision had been transformed. He pushed through the crowds, surged out the door, and fell to his knees in the snow outside.

"God," he prayed out loud, not caring that others could hear, "I've been so wrong! I've been asking you to fit your plans into my dreams. What was I thinking, God? I should be building my dreams on your plans! I see your plan clearly now, God. Give me the courage to follow your will. I will go wherever you want me to go. I will be whatever you want me to be. I am yours—totally, completely, with nothing held back for myself. Use me, God. Use me to do your work."

As people skirted Nate, he remained in the snow, face upturned in the moonlight, hands held high. It was a moment of transformation like nothing Nate had ever experienced before. After hearing Dr. Zoller's message and being moved by God's Spirit, Nate no longer cared what he wanted from life; his new focus was on what God wanted for his life. And Nate knew exactly what that was: He would go to Bible college and become a missionary in a foreign land.

Throughout his time in the Army, Nate had frequently written long letters to his parents back in Huntingdon, Pennsylvania. That night, after the service at Dr. Zoller's church, Nate wrote to them once again, describing his new understanding of God's plan for his life and expressing the deep joy he was feeling. He told them that after the war was over and his time in the Army was complete, he planned to enroll in Bible college and eventually do God's work in a foreign land. Nate knew so much of his time and energy had been spent chasing after his own dreams and desires; now he wanted the rest of his life to be spent following the roadmap of God's perfect plan.

When Nate returned from his special project in Detroit a few weeks later, he found a letter from his father waiting for him. Inside was an article clipped from the *Sunday School Times*. Nate skimmed the article, then went back and read it carefully from beginning to end. It talked about a new organization called Christian Airmen's Missionary Fellowship (CAMF), recently founded by two former military pilots, Jim Truxton and Betty Greene. Their mission was to use planes and pilots to service missionaries in remote areas, bringing news and supplies and offering necessary transport.

Nate could barely breathe; his heart pounded with excitement. The concept of a missionary pilot was new and thrilling. Could a missionary be a pilot? Could a pilot be a missionary? Was God really offering Nate the opportunity to live his dearest dreams to the fullest while also accomplishing God's will for his life? Could CAMF be the answer to Nate's prayers? There was only one way to find out.

Preparation for the Journey

Without hesitation, Nate grabbed a pen and paper and wrote a letter to Jim Truxton, president of Christian Airmen's Missionary Fellowship (CAMF). Nate outlined his background as both a pilot and a mechanic. He told Jim Truxton that he had surrendered his life and all his abilities to do God's will. Nate wrote that he was answering the call for Christian airmen to work in the service of the Lord. Jim Truxton's response was rapid and enthusiastic: Nate was just the kind of guy they needed!

Before he could become fully involved with CAMF, however, Nate had to finish his military service. He was eventually transferred from Indiana to California, where he served at two bases before his discharge from the Army. During this time, Nate was active in churches wherever he lived. He also led Bible studies for his fellow soldiers, read God's Word faithfully, and spent hours alone with God in prayer and meditation. It was perfect preparation for his future ministry.

Over the Thanksgiving holiday, Nate visited an old friend, Joanna Montgomery, in a nursing school in Los Angeles. She greeted Nate warmly when he entered the lobby of the nurses' residence.

"How have you been, Nate?" Joanna asked with a smile. "We've been praying for you. And I always enjoy reading your letters."

Nate grinned. "Well, I'm glad I can amuse you, even if only a little bit. So, how's life in nursing school?"

Joanna and Nate stood in the lobby, chatting and reminiscing about old times. As they talked, the door swung open and a pretty girl bustled into the lobby. Her name was Marjorie Farris, and she was good friends with Joanna Montgomery. In fact, she had read many of Nate's letters, and she recognized him immediately from a snapshot Nate had enclosed in one of his letters. Her heart skipped a beat as she saw the tall blond soldier in the crisp uniform. They talked for a while, but Marj had work to do, so she excused herself to finish her ironing in the basement of the building.

As Marj ironed as fast as she could, she remembered Nate saying he was headed to San Bernadino, California that weekend. Marj finished her work quickly and rushed back upstairs. Nate was still there, talking with Joanna.

"Excuse me," Marj offered, "but I couldn't help thinking you might need a ride to San Bernadino this weekend. My cousin and I are headed that way. Would you like to go with us?"

Nate hesitated. "I wouldn't want to be a bother."

"It's no bother at all," Marj said, beaming. "We're going to San Bernadino anyway, and you need a ride. It seems like the most logical solution."

"Well, okay then. Thanks!" Nate said with a smile.

Although Nate turned down the invitation to spend the weekend with Marj and her cousin, an important friendship had been established. At that point, Nate had no idea that he would spend the next few years writing to Marj before they finally married in 1948. Even when Nate wasn't actively seeking God, God was working in his life, preparing a perfect plan for him.

Another California experience that helped Nate see the hand of God came in December, when Nate and two Army friends headed up to Yosemite National Park for a few days of rest and relaxation. The winter air was damp and cold, and fog draped itself around trees and over buildings. Nate's buddies wanted to putter around at the base of the mountain, exploring the canyon floor. But Nate had his heart set on climbing up to Glacier Point. Since his friends were not interested, he decided to make the climb alone, with only a few layers of clothing on and a handful of peanut chews in his pocket.

The rangers at the base of the trail told Nate the trail was officially closed, but he was welcome to try the climb if he wanted to.

"There are a few tricky spots," the rangers warned him. "And it is dangerous to go alone."

"That's okay," Nate said. "I like a good challenge. Besides, I've been stuck in a barracks full of men for the last three years. Solitude sounds heavenly."

"Well, if you make it to the top," one ranger said, "tell Douglas Whiteside we say hello."

"Oh, I'll make it to the top," Nate assured them. "But who is Douglas Whiteside?"

"He's a nature lover and photographer," the ranger answered. "For reasons I totally don't understand, he is spending the winter alone at the Glacier Point Inn."

"Sounds like an interesting fellow," Nate said. "I'll be sure to look him up when I get there, and I'll tell him you said hello."

With that, Nate started up the trail. The first part was easy going, but as he climbed out of the fog in the valley, the gentle drizzle turned to stinging sleet. Nate was soon damp and cold and tired, but he was determined to press onward. The sleet became pellets of snow, then driving flakes that accumulated quickly on the narrow path. Nate knew he should turn back, but he was sure he must be nearing the Glacier Point Inn, and he hoped to stop there and wait out the storm. He plodded along as the dusting of snow became an inch, then three inches, then six inches. He was stopping every five minutes to catch his breath, and he was eating snow to stay hydrated. The meager supply of peanut chews had been finished long before.

In his pain and exhaustion, Nate wasn't thinking straight. He was lost, stumbling through the snow recklessly toward what he hoped was Glacier Point. The outline of the trail had long since vanished, and when he ran across fresh bear tracks, Nate began to realize the true danger of his situation. With sudden clarity of mind, he lifted his eyes to the sky.

"God," Nate cried out, tears running down his cheeks, "I need you! Thank you for being with me. Thank you for sending your Son to bring me salvation. Thank you for your Word, and your promises. Thank you that I can be sure my home is in heaven."

Nate paused, as quiet sobs shook his body. He understood he might die in the growing darkness. But he didn't feel afraid. A sense of God's peace washed over him and Nate realized his life was in God's hands, no matter what.

"I will serve you with my life," Nate prayed aloud. "It doesn't matter to me whether you choose to take my life here on this mountain or serving you in a foreign land someday. Whatever your will might be, I will serve you."

Nate took a deep breath and plodded on, struggling against nearly fifteen inches of snow. Then, through the blowing snow, Nate glimpsed a phone line. With renewed hope and joy, he followed the line to the Glacier Point Inn. Nate pounded on the door with every ounce of strength left in him. Within seconds, the door swung open.

"Hello," Nate said. "Are you Doug Whiteside?"

"Yes," the puzzled man said. "Who are you?"

"My name is Nate Saint," Nate replied, pushing past him and collapsing in a chair. "And the rangers at the bottom of the trail say hello."

Doug Whiteside cared for Nate while he spent a day recovering from his trek. On that hike, God had taught Nate more about surrender, more about perseverance, and more about facing fear with faith. These were lessons that Nate pondered as he headed down the mountain a few days later on a pair of borrowed snowshoes. They were lessons that would stay with Nate for the rest of his life.

In February 1946, when his military service was complete, Nate applied to Bible college to help prepare him for his work with CAMF. Although he was too late to enroll right away, Nate felt taking a few years of Bible college courses would make him a better missionary. Since it would be a few months before he could start actively studying, Nate left California and headed home to Huntingdon, Pennsylvania to spend some time with his family. In his blissful relaxation, Nate was unaware that CAMF faced a new challenge in Mexico, a challenge that would catapult Nate into missionary service much sooner than he expected.

The Adventure Begins

Deep in southern Mexico, two CAMF pilots had crashed a small biplane when landing at an isolated jungle airstrip on CAMF's first mission for Wycliffe Bible Translators. Both of the left wings, the propeller, and the landing gear had severe damage. Though no one was hurt, the crash grounded CAMF's only plane in southern Mexico and brought missionary aviation work in the area to a complete stop. CAMF president Jim Truxton could only think of one person who was qualified to solve the problem: Nate Saint.

When Jim Truxton contacted him, Nate hesitated. He didn't want to postpone going to college, but it seemed like God was opening a door for Nate to use his abilities to make a difference. So Nate did the only thing he knew how to do when he felt confused: he prayed. After praying for a few days about the decision, Nate sent an answer to Jim Truxton at CAMF headquarters in California. Nate said he could be ready to leave for Mexico in two weeks.

Two days later, Katherine Saint brought a letter into the kitchen where Nate was sitting. "This came for you, son," she said.

"Thanks, Mom," Nate said, giving her hand a squeeze and taking the letter from her.

Katherine Saint smiled. It was so good to have Nate home. She studied his face as a frown spread across his lips and his eyebrows drew together.

"This can't be right," Nate said, shaking his head.

"What is it, Nate?"

"Well," Nate said, "you know that I accepted the job in Mexico for CAMF, right?"

Katherine nodded. "And we are so proud of you for doing the Lord's work."

"I told them I could leave for Mexico in two weeks," Nate went on. "But this train ticket has me leaving Philadelphia in three days! I can't be ready to leave in three days."

Katherine sat down and looked deeply into Nate's eyes. "Do you trust God, son?"

"Of course, Mom," Nate answered.

"Then trust that he is in control of this situation. He knows when you are supposed to arrive in Mexico. And you want to be in the center of his will, don't you, son?"

Nate smiled and kissed his mother's forehead as he rose from his chair. "Of course I do, Mama. As always, you are wise."

"So, where are you going?" Katherine asked as Nate headed for the stairs.

"If I'm leaving in three days, I better get cracking with my preparations!" Nate called back as he disappeared toward his room.

Three days sped by in a crazy blur. Nate scurried to get his passport, sell some of his belongings, and spend precious moments with his family. Nate's family were sad to see him leaving again after such a short time at home, but they all wholeheartedly supported Nate's desire to be a part of this new adventure for God.

With all the pieces in place, Nate said his goodbyes and boarded the train in Philadelphia. All of his belongings and forty pounds of tools were stuffed into an oversized duffel bag. Although he felt a little shaken and scared by all the new things that lay before him, Nate was also incredibly excited. This was his first missionary journey! He could not wait to see what God was going to do through him.

As the train chugged its way across the Midwest toward the Texas border with Mexico, Nate began to think over the details of his situation. He wondered what kind of damage he might need to repair on the airplane that crashed. Jim Truxton had only told Nate that his skills were needed to make the repairs. Nate also wondered how he would communicate in Mexico since he spoke no Spanish. He suddenly realized what a great problem that posed.

As always, God was fully aware of Nate's problems. On the last day of the train ride, four young Mexican men boarded the train and sat near Nate. When he overheard them speaking a foreign language, Nate knew it was Spanish and these men were a direct answer to his prayers.

"Excuse me," Nate said to the young men. "Do you speak English?"

"Si," said one of the men. "Yes, we do. Did you need something?"

Nate explained his circumstances. "I guess I need a crash course in Spanish," he admitted. "Can you help me?"

The young men laughed and agreed to help Nate learn a few basic phrases to help him get by. Over the next few hours, as the Mexican border crept nearer and nearer, the four young men made Nate recite simple Spanish phrases over and over until he felt comfortable. They also huddled with Nate over an old map of Mexico and helped him find his final destination. It was a city called Tuxtla Gutierrez, a tiny dot on the map, hidden deep in southern Mexico, almost to the border with Guatemala.

When Nate reached the Texas border town of Laredo, he followed instructions from CAMF and located the new airplane propeller he was supposed to carry into Mexico. It was waiting for him in a customs warehouse, but the Mexican border agents would not let him carry it into Mexico. After a few harried phone calls to Jim Truxton, Nate was told to ship the propeller into the country by train. Once the propeller was shipped, Nate boarded a plane for a direct flight to Mexico City.

At the bustling Mexico City airport, Nate shouldered his duffel bag and looked around for a friendly face. All around him were strangers speaking Spanish. Nate felt overwhelmed and a little lost. Then a smiling woman appeared by his side.

"You must be Nate Saint," she said.

Nate was relieved. "You speak English," he said with a grin. "And yes, I'm Nate Saint."

"Welcome to Mexico, Mr. Saint. I'm Betty Greene, CAMF pilot and co-founder."

"Please, Ms. Greene, call me Nate," he said. "It's great to meet you."

Betty shook Nate's outstretched hand. "Well, Nate, it's good to meet you too. And you can call me Betty. Shall we go?"

She waved toward the broad doors and Nate nodded. They found their way outside and Betty turned to him and smiled.

"Here's our ride," she said, waving toward a bus that was packed with people. Bags and young men hung from the outside as well, and the bus looked like it was held together by the patches of rust that dappled the frame. Eager faces peered out the windows at the two foreigners standing beside the bus.

Nate was doubtful. "Can we fit?"

"Oh, they'll make room for me inside," she assured him. "But you had better find a spot on the rear bumper. Give your duffel bag to that man over there so he can put it on top. Then hang on; they've been known to drive a bit crazily on these roads."

Nate watched Betty elbow her way into the crowd on the bus, finding a spot near the front door. He reluctantly handed his duffel bag to a wiry young man who flung it onto the roof. As the bus began to pull away, two young men hauled Nate up. They shimmied sideways so he could balance one foot on the two-inch pipe that served as a rear bumper. As the bus wound through the narrow streets, Nate cringed with every bump and turn. He breathed a deep sigh of relief and thankfulness when they finally creaked to a stop at their destination.

During his time in Mexico City, Nate learned a lot from Betty. She told him the details of the missionary aviation program in southern Mexico. She explained the challenges of the terrain and the rugged jungle airstrips. She gave advice about supplies Nate might need and problems he might face. But just like Jim Truxton, Betty Greene offered no details about the damage to the plane that Nate would be repairing, even though she had been on board at the time of the crash. Nate was very curious about what he would face, but he didn't want to seem too nosy, so he said nothing.

On his last day in Mexico City, Nate went shopping with Betty to pick up a few last minute items he might need in Tuxtla Gutierrez. Then it was time to say goodbye.

"Thank you for all your help," Nate told Betty, extending his hand.

"You're welcome," Betty replied, shaking Nate's outstretched hand. "I hope my experience helps you at least a little."

"I'm sure it will help," Nate said. "After all, you're the expert in this area. I'm just the mechanic."

"Well, I wish you all the best on the repairs," Betty said. "We'll be praying for you."

"Thanks," Nate said, turning to go. "Take care."

Nate boarded a small plane to Tuxtla Gutierrez. He was finally on his way to the city where he would begin his work. He was excited by the new experience and eager to start the project. As the plane circled in the deep blue sky and descended to the busy little airport, Nate thanked God that his skills would soon be used in missionary service.

While the main airport and Pan-American Highway were crowded and modern, the actual town of Tuxtla Gutierrez was a portal to the past. Stately old buildings stood quietly around an open plaza where people strolled to marimba music on Saturday evenings. The people were laid back and traditional in their attitudes, their attire, their food, and their festivities. Nate immediately felt welcomed to the community.

As Nate stepped out of the airport, local drivers were lined up to take passengers to their destinations. Nate stopped by a rickety old sedan.

"Where do you want to go?" the driver asked in Spanish.

Nate handed him a paper with directions that Betty had written. In broken Spanish, Nate asked, "Can you take me here?"

"Si," the driver answered with a smile.

He motioned for Nate to get in. Nate threw his duffel bag onto the back seat and loaded his box of supplies beside it. Then he climbed into the car. He was headed to his new home.

The new house was typical for Tuxtla Gutierrez. It was just off the main street of town. The house was one room, with a high roof and smooth, cool walls. There was no bathroom, and the shower was in the back yard. But Nate wasn't worried. He just wanted to get to work on the plane. That was what he had come for.

After settling in a bit and having a good night's sleep, Nate made his way to the sleepy local airport where the damaged plane was parked. It was much smaller and quieter than the main airport for Tuxtla Gutierrez. He quickly found the hangar where the damaged plane was supposed to be. The man who owned the hangar opened the doors and sunlight streamed into the gloomy space.

Nate had expected to see a biplane with damaged landing gear and maybe a splintered propeller. He had planned to find a basic repair job that would take him a few weeks of diligent work. But as he stepped into the hangar and his eyes adjusted to the dimness, Nate's heart sank and his eyes bulged. He couldn't believe what he was seeing!

Tools and Tricks and Getting Sick

"What is this?" Nate asked the owner of the hangar.

"This is what they left with me," the man answered, shrugging his shoulders. "What did you expect to find?"

Nate didn't answer right away. He walked over to the corner of the hangar. Two whole wing panels—or what was left of the wing panels—were jammed into a bushel basket. Beside the basket were pieces of wing struts and landing gear. Everything was stacked up and mixed together.

"Well," Nate finally answered, running a hand over his face. "I expected to find a plane. Where is the plane?"

The owner of the hangar laughed. "The plane is still on the airstrip at El Real, where the crash happened. How would they get the plane here?"

Nate hadn't thought of that. "Well, how far is it to El Real?"

"More than eighty miles," the man answered. "And it is deep in the jungle. You cannot work on the plane there. The work must be done here."

Now Nate understood why Jim and Betty did not give him the full story on the condition of the plane.

He would have turned down the job in an instant. Nate believed in God's power to do anything, but he wasn't sure anyone could fix this plane, at least not to the point of flying again. He paced the floor of the hangar while the owner returned to his work. Nate had no idea where to start on this overwhelming project.

When the initial shock had passed, Nate took a deep breath and began to formulate a plan for recreating the battered plane. He decided he would have to rebuild the wing panels in Tuxtla Gutierrez and fly them to the airstrip at El Real when they were finished. Then he would reassemble the plane in the jungle and fly it off the airstrip and back to the city where CAMF pilots could reclaim it. It was a big job, but Nate claimed God's promises to strengthen him.

One by one, Nate examined the broken pieces. There was so much work to do, and Nate knew he couldn't do it all by himself. He hired a Mexican cabinet maker named Santiago to help him. Santiago spoke no English, and Nate's Spanish consisted of counting to thirteen and asking basic questions, so communication was difficult at first. But they learned from each other and communicated in pictures when necessary. Nate also read passages from a Spanish Bible to a Mexican schoolboy who would come by his house. As the plane slowly came together, Nate's Spanish vocabulary grew and his confidence expanded.

All day, every day, Nate and Santiago worked on reconstructing the wing panel at the airport. The repair required a great deal of creativity and ingenuity. Nate tackled the problem just as he had undertaken his childhood building projects.

"I think we need to change the design over here," Nate said, pointing to a section Santiago was working on.

"How are we changing it?" Santiago asked.

"Let's try this," Nate suggested.

He sketched out a new idea on a large sheet of paper. Santiago watched over Nate's shoulder, tipping his head and nodding. When Nate finished drawing, Santiago studied the new diagram.

"Yes," he said. "This could work."

It was a conversation that played itself out over and over again as the men worked together, trying to recreate the two left wings of the biplane. They often tore sections apart and rebuilt them several times, trying to get the aerodynamics just right. Nate understood that the wings had to be perfect if the plane was going to fly safely again. His perfectionistic and cautious nature pushed him to get every detail exactly as it should be.

When work was done for the day, Nate headed home to his little one-room house. It was made of adobe and tile, with no windows and two doors. The doors were cut in half, allowing the top and bottom to swing separately. Nate wondered why the houses in his neighborhood often had the bottom part of the door shut while the top was left open for air and light.

He soon found out. One afternoon, when Nate had both parts of both doors open for fresh air, a burro walked in through the back door! It looked around and paused for a few minutes, then exited through the front door. After that, Nate kept the bottom parts of the doors closed to prevent uninvited visitors.

At night, the uninvited visitors came regardless of doors and walls. There was a space between the walls and the roof, and the darkness brought all kinds of creatures into the house. Nate slept beneath mosquito netting, but he would often awake to hear bats flying around in the house. He would also find the netting covered with bugs as long as his thumb and twice as wide. There was no stopping the nightly invasion, so Nate learned to sleep through most of it. God was teaching him to have peace in spite of his circumstances.

Another challenge Nate faced with his house was the bathroom facilities. Since the house was so small and lacked running water, Nate's bathroom was an oversized cactus in the back yard. His shower was outdoors too, constructed from discarded packing crates. It had only three sides, so modesty was virtually impossible. For the first few weeks, Nate bathed in the chilly darkness, trying to avoid being seen. But he soon learned this was an unavoidable part of life in southern Mexico, and no one was bothered by it— except maybe him! Over time, Nate adapted to this change, and to nearly all of the dramatic changes from the life he was used to at home in the United States.

The one change that Nate did not adapt to was the food in Mexico. He hated the tortillas that were served with every meal, and he struggled to swallow the local dishes. Finally, Nate settled into an odd and unbalanced diet of eggs, tomatoes, and bananas. Weight slid off his already slim frame until he was a walking skeleton. He was hungry and tired, and he was working long days with no relief. During this time, Santiago quit working for Nate, and he found himself all alone and facing the repairs and a host of physical challenges all on his own.

Nate's body was not used to the Mexican viruses and bacteria, and his diet did not provide much strength to fight disease. He was exhausted and sick a great deal of the time, and he was not making much progress on fixing the plane. He often found himself confined to bed for days at a time, praying desperately for help. One morning, in the gray light of dawn, Nate lay on the floor of his little house, too weak to climb back into bed after a night of violent illness. With tears in his eyes, he feebly cried out to God.

"God," he prayed in a hoarse whisper, "I came here to answer your call. I want to give you my best, but I just can't go on like this anymore. I need help, God. Please, send someone to help me. I have to finish this job, but I need you to strengthen me."

As he lay there on the dirt floor, Nate felt a wave of calm rush through his spirit. He knew without a doubt that God was going to answer his prayer. He had total faith that God would send someone to come and help him in his work. But Nate was isolated in his little house in a little Mexican village in the middle of nowhere. Who would know where to find him? Who would even know he needed help?

An Answer to Prayer

God's answer to Nate's prayers came in the form of Wycliffe missionary Phil Baer, who left his own work to come and help when a local told him about Nate's troubles. Phil had no mechanical or flight experience, but he could cook and clean, which was what Nate needed most. While Nate worked on the plane, Phil kept the little house clean and made hearty, tasty, nourishing meals for Nate. Within a few weeks, Nate was feeling stronger and healthier, and he was gaining weight again.

Due to a disagreement with the owner of the hangar at the Tuxtla Gutierrez airport, Nate had moved the wing pieces to his house and continued the rebuilding there. The tiny building was stuffed to capacity with two men and an airplane wing, but Nate and Phil stepped around each other and climbed over the wing to get things done. Phil helped with the building whenever he could, but the rest of the time he focused on keeping Nate healthy. This enabled Nate to do his work more quickly and efficiently.

One night, Nate and Phil sat outside, watching the last bits of sunset light drain from the sky. Nate turned to Phil and grinned.

"I finished my work on the wing tonight," he told Phil.

"Congratulations, Nate! That's great news."

"Well, I couldn't have done it without your help," Nate admitted. "It's been a rough journey. I'm so glad God answered my prayers by sending you."

"Whatever happened with that part that didn't match the wing or the factory specifications? Did you fix it?" Phil asked.

"No, not yet," Nate said. "I decided it would be best to fix that at the plane in El Real. That way I can construct something that exactly matches the existing part on the other wing. I think that will be the best way to make it safe."

Phil nodded. "You would know best. So, what's next?"

"Well," Nate said, "we need to find a skilled bush pilot with a plane big enough to carry us and the parts out to El Real. Know anybody?"

Phil thought for a few moments. "I think I might know a guy," he said. "Do you mind if we bring my wife and baby along?"

"The more the merrier," Nate said with a grin. "So, where do we find this guy?"

"He'll be in town tomorrow, probably at the local bar. He's a scoundrel, but he's a good pilot," Phil said. "Let's get a good night's sleep and I'll take you to meet him first thing in the morning."

The only bush plane in town that was big enough to carry the wing to the airstrip—but still small enough to land at El Real—was piloted by the man Phil knew. He was a surly, drunken man who had no interest in doing something to help their cause.

"How much can you pay?" he asked.

Nate laid a reasonable stack of bills on the table. The pilot looked at the stack and laughed.

"Try again," he said. "And make it worth my while."

Nate dug in his pockets and removed every cent he had. He piled the money onto the table.

"You're getting closer," the pilot grumbled, "but you've got a ways to go before you even get my attention."

"But that's all I have," Nate protested.

"Here," Phil said, emptying his pockets onto the table as well. "That's all we have between us. Take it or leave it."

The pilot studied the money and the men. He scowled. For a moment he was silent, tipping his head to the side. Then he raked the money toward him and stuck out his hand with a drunken grin.

"Congratulations, fellows," he said, shaking Nate's hand and then Phil's. "You just bought yourself the best bush pilot there is. We'll load up tomorrow morning."

Phil and Nate were penniless, but rejoicing. God had provided a way to get the wing to the plane. They hurried home to prepare everything for transport and move it to the airstrip. When all the pieces were ready to be loaded, they slept fitfully for a few hours. As the sun peeked over the horizon, they headed back to the airstrip.

Phil's wife and baby met them there. The surly pilot helped cram the airplane parts into his plane. Phil's wife climbed in around the parts and held her baby tightly. There was no room for Phil, so he would have to make the eighty-mile journey on foot. After saying goodbye to Phil, Nate climbed into the co-pilot seat and the pilot started the engine.

The overburdened bush plane struggled to get into the air. The pilot tinkered with the controls and swore angrily. As the trees at the end of the runway loomed large, the plane lurched and climbed steeply into the sky, dangerously close to stalling. It skimmed the treetops and leveled off, finally climbing steadily. They were on their way to El Real at last.

The pilot flew hard and fast, pushing the plane to its limits. Nate held his breath for the entire flight. They soared recklessly through narrow passes and swooped crazily above the jungle treetops. When the dog-leg landing strip at El Real came into view, nestled deep within the lush surroundings, Nate silently prayed for a speedy and safe end to their perilous journey.

The bush plane screeched safely to a stop on the ground, and the passengers climbed out. The wing parts were unloaded and piled by the side of the runway. With barely a goodbye, the pilot jumped back into the cockpit and buzzed down the runway and into the sky, headed toward Tuxtla Gutierrez. Nate was finally ready to finish his work.

Nate turned his attention to the wreckage of the plane, nestled in the bushes just off the airstrip. It was in much worse condition than he had expected. The fuselage was battered and scarred from the crash. But when Nate tried the ignition, the engine roared to life. Filled with hope, Nate wasted no time constructing and assembling the new wing and fixing the damaged parts. He was determined to make the crumpled plane as good as new.

Nate's excitement grew as the refurbished biplane came together. Hard days and nights blurred together in the mosquito-infested jungle. As he neared completion of one repair, he often found several more that needed to be done. One day he found that mud wasps had built a nest in the fuel tank and throughout the fuel lines. Nate lost an exhausting full day of work trying to flush out the fuel system. But persistent as ever, Nate pushed on, determined to get the job done.

When Phil arrived to help, Nate often discussed his planned repairs aloud, checking the validity of his ideas, which were often an unusual blend of innovation and improvisation.

"We're out of fabric, so I think I'll use these bed sheets to finish the fuselage," Nate told Phil one sweltering afternoon. "They're strong and should be aerodynamic. But I need something to fix this landing gear drag strut. Any ideas?"

Phil tipped his head and thought. "What does it need to look like?"

Nate pointed to the other landing gear drag strut. "Like that. Straight and solid, and definitely sturdy enough to hold the weight of the plane under the trauma of landing."

"Maybe a car part," Phil suggested.

"That's it!" Nate cried. He dug through his bag of odds and ends and came out with a Ford V-8 steering column. "This will be perfect!"

With imagination and a healthy dose of inspiration, Nate pieced the plane back together. He rebuilt both familiar and unfamiliar parts with the same care and consideration he had used to construct airplane models during his childhood. In fact, during the repairs, he often thought back on those long, lazy summer days when he made airplanes and boats and railroads. Nate had not realized that God was using even those childhood moments of fun to prepare Nate for missionary service.

The day the repairs were completed was a day for celebration. Nate sent word to CAMF, and pilot George Wiggins came and tested the plane extensively. With George's hearty approval, the job was declared done, and Nate was cleared to return to the United States. He bid a reluctant farewell to Phil and began his journey home.

Nate's experiences in Mexico changed the course of his life. He knew more than ever what God's plan was for his life. The experiences also changed the course of missionary aviation in positive and important ways. CAMF directors realized that missionary pilots needed to have at least a basic understanding of airplane mechanics. This knowledge could prove invaluable when a pilot found himself stranded in a remote part of the jungle. Missionary aviation was a specialized field that required special personnel.

With all his heart, Nate was ready to become a missionary aviator, but he felt Bible college would enable him to better share God's Word with others. While he was visiting CAMF in Los Angeles on his way home from Mexico, Nate received word that he had been accepted to Wheaton College for January 1947. He hurried home for a quick visit and then made his way to Wheaton, Illinois, where he plunged headlong into his studies.

Although Nate was never much of a scholar, he diligently tried to do his best to succeed in school. He was determined to become as skilled in ministry as he was with airplanes. He couldn't wait to finish his training and continue his work in missionary aviation. But while he was in school, Nate learned he and his skill set were in high demand. He received offers to fly for various missionary agencies in Mexico, New Guinea, and South America. On his knees, Nate sought God's guidance with a single question: God, where do you want me to go?

A Whole New World

As Nate prayed for knowledge of God's will, doors began to open in his life. First, over Christmas break, Nate proposed to his old friend, Marj Farris, who he had met when she was still in nursing school in California. They had exchanged many letters over the years, and Nate had visited Marj when he returned to CAMF headquarters after his trip to Mexico. He had no doubts that Marj was the girl God wanted him to marry. And he was right. Marj happily accepted his proposal. She even moved from San Francisco to Illinois to be near Nate as they planned their wedding.

Marj and Nate knew their lives together would be lived out on the mission field, but as they prayed over the weeks following their engagement, they were unsure which field to go to. Ecuador and New Guinea both offered extensive opportunities in new missionary aviation programs. Nate knew there were lost souls on both fields, and he knew he could not be in two places at once. Ecuador and New Guinea were on opposite sides of the globe, and Nate longed to know for sure which one held God's future for him.

A few weeks after Christmas, God's direction became amazingly clear. The Dutch government—

which had authority in New Guinea—was holding up work permits for missionary aviators. It could be months or even years before missionaries were allowed into the country. Meanwhile, the need in Ecuador was dire and immediate, with many tribes that had never heard the gospel at all. The decision was easily made; Nate and Marj were headed for Ecuador.

In late January, Nate came to Marj with a new plan.

"Dear," he said, "I think we should leave college after this semester."

"You mean at the end of the month?" Marj asked in surprise.

"Yep," Nate answered. "I think we should move up the wedding to the spring. It just seems to me like I've learned all I can learn. Souls are dying in Ecuador without ever knowing Jesus."

"That's true, Nate, but are you sure this is God's will? It's not just your idea?"

Nate sat beside Marj and took her hand. "I have prayed about this long and hard, Marj. We can do more good in Ecuador telling those who have never heard than we can teaching Sunday School here in Illinois to kids who have heard the story a million times."

She smiled at him. "Okay. I trust your judgment, and I know you're in tune with God's will for our lives. So, a wedding in March or April, maybe?"

Nate grinned. "You always understand me. I think that's why God sent you to me. But I don't want to make any decisions about the future until I talk with Charlie

Mellis. He's coming up in a couple of weeks. We'll talk to him, pray together, and then make our plans."

In mid-February, Charlie Mellis, recently-elected president of Missionary Aviation Fellowship (MAF)—the new name for CAMF—came to Illinois to discuss the missionary aviation needs in Ecuador with Nate and Marj. Charlie had been to Ecuador and had been in contact with several missionaries there. He painted a vivid picture of life in Ecuador and the challenges the missionaries faced.

"There are dozens of tribes nestled into the jungles," Charlie told them. "Some are headhunters; others are cannibals. None have heard the gospel. And these missionaries are trying to reach them."

"But how?" Nate asked. "Are there roads or some kind of thoroughfares?"

"Some trails exist," Charlie told them, "but missionaries must often cut through the jungle and make their own paths, taking days or even weeks to reach civilization. Can you imagine the impact an aviation ministry could have on these missionaries and their works?"

Nate could imagine it. "We could drop medicine, food, and news of the outside world," he said, his voice building with excitement. "We could use radios to communicate, build jungle airstrips, and provide physical and medical aid."

"Yes," Charlie agreed. "And fellowship. That's one of the things these missionaries crave the most. They need fellow helpers in the truth, as the Bible says."

"Do these missionaries have wives?" Marj asked.

"Oh, yes," Charlie answered. "Several of them are married and raising children in the jungles."

"But isn't it dangerous?" Marj wondered.

"I suppose so," Charlie said. "There are bugs, animals, diseases, and violent tribes that don't like outsiders. But these missionaries are trusting God to protect them, and they are praying for missionary aviators like you to help revolutionize the ministry in Ecuador."

Nate and Marj had heard all they needed to hear. For the first time, they fully realized what a missionary pilot would mean to God's faithful servants in Ecuador: supplies, medical care, efficient transport to remote areas, and contact and fellowship with the outside world. Nate and Marj were ready to leave the comforts of the world they knew and move to a world where God could use them in a mighty way. It was obvious God needed them in Ecuador as soon as possible.

In answer to God's call, Nate and Marj decided to get married that very month and head for Ecuador immediately. They were eager to do God's work. They left college, contacted Marj's parents, and left for New York. On Valentine's Day, February 14, 1948, Nate and Marj were married in the Baptist church in Manhasset, New York. They were surrounded by friends and family and filled with joy and excitement about the adventure that waited for them thousands of miles away.

After a brief honeymoon, Nate and Marj spent the next six months criss-crossing the United States to raise money for their mission work. Churches would pledge monthly gifts to support the missionary aviation endeavors. These monthly gifts would be used to buy fuel and supplies, as well as to finance food, housing, and building projects. In every church, Nate and Marj presented the need in Ecuador and made an impassioned plea for help so they could get to the field and get started on the job God had for them to do.

When they finally had enough money, Nate and Marj said goodbye to their families and began the adventure of a lifetime. The night before they left, Nate sat with Marj and watched the sunset.

"Well, tomorrow's the big day," he said. "Are you nervous?"

Marj smiled at him. "Of course not. I have perfect peace about God's plan. I only wish I could travel with you."

"I know," Nate said, turning toward her. "But it's better this way. It's safer for you and the baby to travel on the commercial airline. The trip is shorter and the seats are way more comfortable."

"But I barely know Betty Truxton," Marj said. "I'm sure the baby and I would be fine flying with you."

Nate patted Marj's growing belly affectionately. "I know you're a tough cookie. But I really need to help Jim get this plane down to Ecuador. It's the plane we'll be using, so I need to be familiar with it. And Betty could use the company."

"And you'll be there when I get there?"

"I'll be in Ecuador before you ever leave the United States. And I'll get started making a home for us. Do you believe me?" Nate's voice was gentle.

"Of course I believe you," Marj said with a smile. "You always tell me the truth. And you're right. This is just the first step in our journey together. I can't wait to see what God has in store."

The next morning, September 8, 1948, Marj and Betty stood on the tarmac and waved goodbye as Nate and Jim climbed into the MAF airplane that would launch missionary aviation in Ecuador. After a four-day flight with multiple stops for rest and refueling, the little plane landed in Quito, the capital of Ecuador, on September 12. By the time Marj and Betty arrived by commercial airline on September 16, Nate and Jim were already on their way to the Shell Oil outpost at Shell Mera. The foundation for the future was at their fingertips.

Starting Out at Shell Mera

Nestled in the Andes Mountains, Shell Mera was a base camp for Shell Oil. It had a near-perfect climate and an excellent airstrip that would serve as the MAF headquarters in Ecuador. It was in close proximity to several missionaries and only a short flight away from many others. In fact, several Shell Oil sites would eventually become missionary outposts, but Shell Mera was the first and the most centrally located.

The first missionary aviation flight went out on Nate's first day at Shell Mera. He soon learned the aerial green map that was the jungle, tracing rivers, trails, and the camps and villages that pockmarked the emerald landscape. He delivered supplies and equipment to remote airstrips carved out of the leafy canopy. He flew medicine to sick villagers and missionaries. He transported the badly injured and very ill out of the jungle to modern medical care. Journeys Nate could make in minutes took hours or days on foot.

Missionary aviation wasn't Nate's only focus. Marj was still in Quito until Nate could build a house that would be comfortable for her and the baby that was coming soon. With a crew of a half-dozen men, building on a house at the Shell Mera site began immediately. They spent their days constructing a solid house that was big enough to shelter guests and missionaries that would pass through. They added innovations that were unheard of in Ecuador: a shower, a washing machine, and even a hydroelectric power plant. And at night, they sat around a campfire, ate, and talked about missionary life.

One night, a visiting missionary joined them. He shared information that would change Nate's life course forever.

"Have you heard about the crazy tribe deep in the jungle?" the missionary asked. "They set a whole new standard for savage behavior."

"What do you mean?" Nate asked, his curiosity piqued.

"Well," the missionary said, "the Quichua Indians call them 'Aucas,' which means 'savages' in the Quichua language. The locals say these Aucas have lived in isolation for more than 300 years. They attack and often kill anyone who tries to make contact with them."

"They just kill them? Just like that? With no reason or warning?" Nate wondered.

"So I've heard," the missionary told him. "Now, I haven't seen them myself, because no one knows exactly where they live. They move around a lot. But some oil folks stumbled across an Auca village a few years back and they were all slaughtered. A search party found their bodies weeks later. By then the Aucas had moved on to a different camp."

As Nate listened to the tales the missionary told, his heart felt tight within his chest. There was a whole tribe with no contact with the outside world. There was not a single member of the tribe who had heard God's Word. There was no way for them to hear because of their hostility. But there was only one remedy for their savage behavior: transformation through Christ. Staring into the flickering campfire, Nate silently prayed that God would someday give him a chance to take the gospel to the Auca people.

With long, hard days and extensive teamwork, the house was finally ready for Marj in late October. Nate brought her from Quito to Shell Mera, and she immediately started settling into the sprawling house. She spent her days putting finishing touches in each room and helping Nate with overall improvements and innovations he dreamed up. They also unpacked belongings that had been crated up and shipped to Ecuador months earlier. It was almost like Christmas, rediscovering long-forgotten belongings. Still, Nate's first duty was to care for and minister to the jungle missionaries.

To help in the aviation ministry, a short-wave radio was installed at Shell Mera. A smaller radio was installed in Nate's plane. Over time, many of the missionaries also set up radios. This created inter-connectivity throughout the jungle, easing communication and making it much easier to understand and respond to the needs of the missionaries. The new system made the base at Shell Mera a hub for messages, requests, needs, and rejoicing.

By early December, the house was just how Marj wanted it, and she had to move back to Quito. She was almost ready to give birth to her first child, and there were modern hospitals and skilled doctors there in the capital city. She had to go alone, however, since Nate could not be spared from the missionary work. It was a difficult time for them, and as soon as he could get away for a few days, Nate made a weekend visit to Quito.

"It has been so good to see you," Marj said as they sat side-by-side on their last evening together. "I've missed you so much."

"I've missed you, too," Nate said, squeezing her hand. "But there are so many needs to meet. I'm busy from dawn 'til dusk, especially without you there to keep me organized."

Marj laughed. "How soon do you think you can come back to see me?"

"I'll be here as soon as I receive word the baby has been born," Nate promised.

The next morning was December 30, and Nate said goodbye to Marj and headed for the Quito airport. He loaded up some supplies for Shell Mera and several of the missionaries. He also took on two passengers, the wife and son of a missionary doctor.

He did his preflight checks and confirmed flying conditions. Everything was ready to go.

The takeoff was normal as the little plane soared toward the craggy peaks of the Andes. But 200 feet above the runway, the plane hit a violent down-draft. The last thing Nate remembered, the ground was rising rapidly toward the cockpit. He turned the plane into the wind, toward a plowed field. There were the frantic cries of his two passengers, the thud of shifting cargo, and the sickening crunch of crushing metal. Then there was silence and darkness.

The plane was no more than a heap of debris and dirt on the field, but as soldiers from the Ecuadorian Army responded to the crash, they were amazed to find the passengers largely unhurt. They had scratches, cuts, bruises, and a few broken bones, but they would recover. Nate, on the other hand, had severely torn ligaments in his ankle. Worst of all, his back was broken. The doctors wondered if he would ever walk again, let alone fly.

Marj had been called, and she had rushed to the main hospital. She held Nate's hand and tried to comfort him. He cringed in pain and frustration as the doctors put him into a plaster cast. It began at his neck and extended to his upper thighs, holding his body rigid and stiff. It was itchy and uncomfortable, and it kept Nate from doing anything for himself, especially in those first few days.

As he lay in his hospital bed, Nate wondered where God's plan was in the crash. He replayed the scenario over and over again in his mind, wondering if he could have done anything differently. But the down-draft had been an uncontrolled force of nature, something he could not have foreseen or planned for. Still, as a result of the crash, Nate saw opportunities to improve pilot safety. He thanked God that he was alive, but he was also beginning to worry. Would he ever fly again?

Birthing Babies and Ideas

Nine days after the accident, Nate was flown to Panama to be examined by U.S. Military doctors. They did not have good news for Nate. His injuries were more serious than originally thought. But good news did arrive from Quito the next day. Nate was a father! His daughter, Katherine Joan Saint, had just been born. Nate was overjoyed and thankful in spite of the challenges he was facing. God was blessing Nate, and he was sure his ministry wasn't over yet.

By the end of January, Nate rejoined Marj and little Kathy in Quito. He loved the downtime to relax and enjoy his little daughter as he recovered. With God's help, Nate could look at the benefits of his injury instead of feeling sorry for himself. But he was anxious to return to Shell Mera and the work he had come to love. When the doctors finally released him to leave Quito—body cast and all—he and Marj celebrated. They couldn't wait to settle into family life at Shell Mera.

Before he left for home, Nate was asked to speak on the Christian radio station in Quito. He readily accepted the invitation and gave a remarkable sermon over the airwaves. One statement, in particular, painted a clear picture of Nate's motivation for missionary service.

"If God didn't hold back his only Son," Nate said, "but gave Him up to pay the price for our failure and sin, then how can we Christians hold back our lives— the lives He really owns?"

Nate was ready to jump back into missionary work despite the dangers. He was ready to give his life for God's work, if necessary, just like Jesus sacrificed His life for our salvation. Nate saw the need and knew that Jesus was the answer to that need. His whole life was about giving back to God who had given so freely to him.

Upon their arrival back at Shell Mera, Nate and Marj heard tales of what the lack of a plane had meant to the missionaries. Several had trekked for days through the jungle for much-needed supplies. One group of three missionaries walked six days to reach the supply depot at Shell Mera. During their journey, they nearly drowned in a turbulent river, and one became so ill he could barely walk. Stories like these emphasized the vital need for continuing and expanding the missionary aviation program.

Within weeks, a new plane was purchased and specially equipped in Los Angeles and flown to the airstrip at Shell Mera. MAF pilot Hobey Lowrance agreed to fly in Nate's place until he was fully healed and out of his cast. The short-wave radio network was up and running across the jungle, and isolated missionaries routinely called in requests. The daily flights were an immeasurable blessing to the missionaries. It was business as usual again at Shell Mera.

While he was grounded, Nate helped Marj coordinate routine flights and handle emergency calls. In July, an urgent call came in on the short-wave radio.

"Shell Mera, Shell Mera base," Missionary Morrie Fuller said, "Come in, Shell Mera base."

"We're here, Morrie," Nate answered. "What's up?"

"My ten-year-old son, Robert, fell into my circular saw a little bit ago," Morrie said, a hint of panic in his voice.

"Oh, no! How bad is it?" Nate asked.

"Pretty bad. His arm is ripped open. I think we have the bleeding mostly stopped, but he needs a doctor right away."

"Absolutely. Hang in there for a minute, Morrie. I'm going to radio Hobey. He's on his way to another station, but we'll divert him your way."

Morrie Fuller breathed a sigh of relief. "Thanks, Nate. We'll be waiting."

"That's what we're here for," Nate said.

Within minutes, Hobey Lowrance was on his way to the Ahjuana station where the Fullers were waiting. Nate gave Marj the microphone on the short-wave radio and took off on his motorbike, cast and all, to notify the nearby Shell Oil Company doctor. As the doctor prepared to treat Robert, a nurse hurried over to Nate and Marj's house and talked with the Fullers over the radio, getting details about the case. And in only a few hours, Robert had been transported, treated, and was on his way to recovery. Without the missionary aviation team, the trip out of the jungle alone would have taken at least four days of hard walking, and it could have proved deadly for the injured boy. Stories like these reinforced the truth that missionary aviation saved time and lives.

Despite the lifesaving capabilities of aviation, flying over the tangled jungles and craggy peaks of the Andes was also extremely dangerous. In the six months following Nate's accident, there were two crashes within fifty miles of Shell Mera. More than a dozen people were killed in these crashes. While they were not MAF planes that crashed, the statistics still bothered Nate. He knew there must be a way to make flight safer, especially under the tricky conditions they faced. He studied the challenges of flight in the Andes and over the jungles, determined to find solutions to common problems for pilots.

Since Nate couldn't fly during his long months in the body cast, he had some extra time on his hands. When he wasn't working on the house or manning the radio, Nate's boyhood inventive spirit was reawakened. He began sketching safety harness designs to help protect a pilot in a crash. He knew if he had been wearing a safety harness during his crash, his back might not have been broken. When he had perfected a design, he sent drawings back to MAF.

"These are good," Charlie Mellis determined. "Your drawings and explanations of the safety and effectiveness of this harness are very convincing. Have you tested the harness for safety?"

"Of course," Nate answered, detailing what he had done to establish the safety of the new harness design. "I believe a harness like this could save lives and prevent injury."

MAF had Nate's design checked out by engineers, and it was determined to be remarkable. In fact, it was so innovative and effective that harnesses based on Nate's design were soon installed in all MAF planes as well as many private, commercial, and military aircraft. Even in his time of recovery, God was using Nate to do great things.

In addition to the harness design, Nate was also working on an alternate fuel delivery system. Many missionary pilots had crashed over the years because the fuel lines of their planes had become clogged, shutting down the engine. Nate designed an extra fuel tank that attached to the wing of his plane. He built it from items he found lying around the house. One afternoon, Nate came into the kitchen where Marj was cooking.

"Honey, what do you do with your cooking oil cans when they're empty?" Nate asked.

"I put them out back," Marj said, looking puzzled. "Why?"

"Well, I need a couple of them," Nate said. "And do you remember where that balsa wood and brass tubing are?"

"I think they're out in the hangar," Marj said. "Nate, what are you up to?"

"I have an idea, honey, and it's a good one!"

Marj laughed at Nate's exuberance. "Well! I know better than to get in your way when you have an idea. Have fun!"

Nate gave her a quick hug and hurried out the back door. He rigged up two cooking oil cans—one for each wing—and supported the cans with balsa wood. Brass tubing carried the extra fuel into the engine. Using the extra tank would allow the pilot to bypass the regular fuel system and inject the fuel directly. Nate hoped it would help prevent future crashes and engine failures. He couldn't wait until he was flying again so he could test his new invention.

Back in the Saddle Again

Eventually, Nate's long wait was over. The day had arrived for his return to the cockpit. The cast was off, his ankle was healed, and his strength and flexibility were regained. Nate eagerly took the controls of the plane on a brilliantly sunny morning. With Hobey Lowrance beside him, Nate performed a check-out flight, demonstrating his physical and psychological readiness to fly again. After proving his abilities on that flight, Nate was allowed to fly solo. His heart soared as the plane buzzed through the blue sky. He could once again do what God had called him to do.

Nate wasted no time crafting and installing a safety harness for his plane. The next step was attaching and testing the new fuel system. When the invention was in place, Nate took the plane up into the sky. This was the real test of his ingenuity: cutting the engine in flight. He soon had his answer.

"Marj," Nate called over the radio. "Shell Mera base, come in!"

Marj rushed to the microphone. "What is it, Nate? Are you okay?"

"I'm fine," Nate whooped. "It works! My alternate fuel system works."

"How do you know?" Marj asked.

"Well, I took the plane up high," Nate explained, "and then I cut the engine in several different situations. I was trying to simulate all the different problems a pilot could experience. So I tried to cut the engine under all possible conditions."

"Nate!" Marj was shocked. "I guess I'm glad I didn't know you were doing that. Anyway, what happened?"

"It worked! The fuel system functioned perfectly. It never even faltered," Nate said proudly.

He was ecstatic. The alternate fuel system meant a much higher level of safety for jungle pilots. After perfecting the system further, Nate applied for and received a patent on his invention. Within time, Nate Saint's alternate fuel system became standard equipment on all MAF planes.

Nate's inventive mind did not stop at safety devices. He was also inspired to create things that would increase the effectiveness of the ministry aspect of his work. While struggling to communicate with a missionary who did not yet have a short-wave radio, Nate remembered sitting in a college class and watching a pencil dangle at the end of a long string. This image gave him a new idea. He would dangle a message at the end of the line, creating a delivery system that would allow two-way communication.

Using 1500 feet of strong cord and a canvas bucket, Nate devised a way to drop items to remote stations where no airstrip had been cleared. He found if he flew in large circles and then tightened the circles to a very small radius, the bucket eventually hung almost stationary at the end of the cord. It did not swing or sway. This allowed supplies and messages to be exchanged quickly and easily. It was primitive in nature, but it advanced the cause of missionary aviation.

When the bucket drop system had been perfected, Nate added two field telephones to the apparatus. One phone was in the plane, and one was in the bucket. They were connected by a thin wire that snaked along the bucket cord. The perfect opportunity to test the system came when Frank Mathis, a Wycliffe missionary to the village of Arapicos, called for medicine to treat a highly-contagious illness that was spreading through the local population. There was no airstrip in the area, and the bucket drop system would have to be used to deliver the medicine.

With fellow missionary Bob Hart in the plane to help, Nate flew to Arapicos and dropped the bucket into the clearing in the center of the village. Frank Mathis was in the clearing below. When the bucket with the phone dropped to the ground, Frank looked at it with a puzzled expression on his face. Then he picked it up.

"Hello?" he said into the phone.

"Howdy, Frank! This is Bob Hart. How are things down there?"

"How are you doing this?" Frank was amazed by the phone. "This is remarkable."

Bob grinned at Nate up in the cockpit. "It was all Nate's idea, Frank."

"I should have known," Frank said. "He always has great ideas. But in answer to your question, Bob, things are bad down here."

"How bad?" Bob asked.

"Well, a twenty-two-year-old has already died. More are getting sick by the minute. I don't know if I'm in danger or not, but I have to help these people," Frank said.

"What are the symptoms?" Bob asked.

"They are complaining of stomachaches, headaches, leg cramps, cold fingers and toes, and clenched teeth," Frank relayed. "Sound like anything you've heard of?"

"Nate's going to radio back to Quito," Bob told Frank. "We'll be back soon with the appropriate medicine. Hang in there."

Bob reeled in the bucket, and Nate radioed a doctor in Quito, more than 200 miles away. The doctor assured Nate that Frank was not in any danger. Medicine was prescribed, and Nate flew by Shell Mera to pick it up. Within an hour, the medicine had been delivered to Frank and the epidemic was averted. Clearly, the addition of phones to the bucket drop made Nate's system even more efficient and his ministry more effective. In fact, soon after saving the village of Arapicos, Nate and Bob had the opportunity to demonstrate the effectiveness of the bucket phones for the President of Ecuador. God was using Nate to speak to the hearts and needs of rulers and servants alike.

New mission stations were springing up throughout the jungle, serving tribes who had previously been unreached. Nate was often busy flying from the first light of day until darkness settled in between the mountain peaks. Marj manned the radio, purchased needed supplies for the missionaries, and was responsible for coordinating most ministry aspects, including the finances. She was also the busy mother of Kathy, who had grown into an active toddler, and another baby was on the way.

Nate and Marj loved the active life of service God had chosen for them. But as he flew over the jungle in the waning light of evening, Nate found himself often thinking of the Aucas. He could not get the needs of their souls out of his mind. He felt deep within his heart that someday his ministry would be to reach them. Little did he know, a door to the Auca world was about to be opened in his already hectic life.

A Realization and a Recharge

By the time their second child, Steve, was born in January 1951, Nate and Marj's ministry at Shell Mera had expanded unbelievably. New missionaries were coming into the jungle, and while the increased fellowship was a joy, it also meant more outposts to serve through the aviation ministry. The rambling house at Shell Mera was often filled to capacity with travelers passing through. In fact, Nate and Marj and both children often crowded into a single tiny bedroom to make room for those in need of shelter.

The busy days at Shell Mera often began before daylight, with supplies being logged and loaded into Nate's bright yellow plane. By the time breakfast was over, Nate was ready to take off on his first flight of the day. Many days there were five, ten, or even a dozen flights, with short stops for refueling and reloading in between. Nate could—and did—do in a typical day what would have taken forty days on the ground. It was dawn-till-dusk work, but Nate knew he was making a difference and doing the Lord's work.

Amidst the busy pace, there were hours and days for rest and relaxation. During one of these stretches, Nate's older sister, Rachel, came to visit.

She was a missionary, too, working as a translator in a neighboring country. God's direction had led her to leave that country and move to an Ecuadorian hacienda. There she planned to learn some of the native tribal languages. Someday she hoped to translate the Bible into these languages so the tribal people could read God's Word for themselves. Rachel and Nate spent many hours talking about the spiritual needs of the tribal groups.

"Have you heard of the Auca tribe?" Nate asked Rachel.

"No. What's their story?" Rachel replied.

Nate told her what he knew. "Pretty much everybody hates them. Even their neighboring tribes fear them. But I just know in my heart that God wants me to reach them somehow," Nate finished.

"Oh, Thanny," Rachel said, affectionately using his old nickname. "You always did have a heart for seemingly impossible causes. Where do they live?"

"That's just it," Nate said. "No one knows. And when someone does find out, they move again. But as I fly over the jungle, I look for them. I want so much to tell these hated people that there is a God who loves them."

Rachel's eyes shone in agreement and excitement. "I understand exactly how you feel, Thanny. I feel God wants me to spend my life reaching a completely unreached people group."

"This is your tribe, sis," Nate said. "I'm sure of it!"

One afternoon near the end of Rachel's visit, Nate took her up in his plane. He flew her over the lush canopy of trees that covered what neighboring tribes called Auca territory. He waved his hand toward the view out the windshield.

"They're out there somewhere, sis," Nate said. "I can feel it. And God is going to give us the chance someday to reach them with the good news of Jesus."

After such an exciting and uplifting visit, Nate's spirit and drive were rejuvenated, but his body was tired. The feverish pace of the missionary aviation work had taken an extreme physical toll on both Nate and Marj. They were exhausted, and although he was reluctant to admit it, Nate knew they needed a break. He asked MAF to send a couple to replace them at Shell Mera while they took a furlough to the United States to visit their churches and have time with family. In answer, MAF sent Robert and Keitha Wittig to Ecuador. So, in February 1952, Nate and Marj wearily left Shell Mera for some time away.

For the fourteen months they were in the United States, Nate and Marj made Glendale, California their home base. Marj's parents moved nearby to spend time with Kathy and Steve and to care for them while Nate and Marj traveled to raise money and tell congregations about the missionary aviation program in Ecuador. They spoke in churches across the country, from the Pacific Northwest to the Eastern Seaboard. They also presented their ministry on various radio programs across the country. They wanted everyone to know about the work God was doing in Ecuador.

In addition to traveling and presenting their ministry, Nate and Marj took time to be with family and friends. They recognized their need for rest and personal revival. And when they did get too busy in their travels, God gave them ways to slow down. In fact, Nate was forced to rest when he contracted pneumonia in February 1953, not long before their scheduled return to Ecuador. Nate recovered fully, but the bout of pneumonia afforded him some much-needed physical downtime before he plunged back into the rigorous schedule of his Ecuadorian ministry.

While away from Shell Mera, Nate also worked diligently to improve his inventions and increase aviation safety. He perfected his bucket-drop and telephone-wire systems. He fought for the development of planes with two or three motors. He enhanced his alternate fuel tank systems that could bypass fuel lines. He joined with MAF employees and engineers from the North American Aviation Corporation to make airplanes that were safer for flying in the jungles of Ecuador and around the world.

People would often ask Nate why he was so passionate about aviation safety.

"Why not leave it to the engineers and experts?" they would ask.

"Because I know better," Nate would say with confidence.

"But they have studied these things," people would respond. "Doesn't that make them more qualified to make these improvements?"

"Nope," Nate would argue. "They may know what happens to a plane on paper when an engine goes out over an endless jungle. And they may know how to fix it. But I've lived the problem, and I know the paper solutions aren't always the most practical ones. It isn't about solving problems. It's about saving lives."

Headed Back to
Home Sweet Home

By the spring of 1953, Nate and Marj were eager to get back to Shell Mera and the work God had called them to do. MAF decided to send Nate back to Ecuador in a newer, larger plane to expand the Shell Mera fleet. He would fly the plane to Ecuador with co-pilot Henry Carlisle of MAF while Marj, Kathy, and Steve traveled on a commercial airline to Quito. It meant more separation, but it was clearly the best option for both the family and the ministry.

Before leaving California in the new plane, Nate installed a 15-gallon auxiliary fuel tank. It was attached to a bicycle pump that could be used to move the fuel directly into the main tanks if they should run low on fuel. In addition, Nate took a 15-pound bundle of clothes to equip him for whatever conditions they might face on the trip. Beside that bundle was a 23-pound lunch that Marj had packed for them to snack on during the trip. Nate and Henry were well set for their journey!

On the morning of May 29, 1953, Nate and Henry took off on what would be a long and eventful trip to Ecuador. The first night, darkness began to settle before they could find the airstrip that was marked on the map. In desperation, they finally landed on a country road in Mexico. A local rancher helped them pull the plane off the road and behind some low hills. Then the rancher offered food and shelter for the night.

The second night proved even more treacherous than the first. Their landing strip was an old mule trail, rugged and uneven, and barely wide enough to accommodate the wingspan of the plane. After landing, Nate and Henry were met by some gracious locals who offered food and shelter. The two missionaries found the food inedible, but they did manage to choke down some tea. Then they went to sleep on narrow beds with woven rope mattresses. They lay awake in the darkness, listening to the rustle of bugs and creatures scavenging on the floor below. Mosquitoes whined around them and bit them again and again. When the first light of dawn cracked the sky, Nate and Henry were up and headed thankfully to the plane.

The third day, the plane soared lazily through the blue sky, just skirting the western coast of Mexico. Breakers rolled and foamed on the sandy beach far below.

"It sure is beautiful," Henry said, gazing down at the turquoise sea.

"It is indeed," Nate said. "Let's go down for a closer look."

He dropped his altitude to 200 feet. The water was clearly visible, dotted with occasional fishing boats and buoys. Henry raised up and leaned to get a better look out the window.

"Look there, Nate," he said, pointing to several animals frolicking in the water. "Are those dolphins?"

Nate looked out the window and grinned. "Nope, not dolphins."

Henry was puzzled. "Well, what are they then?" he asked.

"Looks to me like they're sharks," Nate answered.

Henry sat back in his seat quickly and looked away from the water. "Perhaps we should go up a bit higher," he said.

Nate laughed and whacked Henry on the shoulder. "Don't worry, friend," he assured the frightened man. "I'm pretty sure sharks can't jump this high."

Within a few hours they turned away from the coast and landed at a well-developed airstrip at the MAF base at Ixtapa. It was a relief to see friendly faces and feast on familiar foods. They settled in for the night in nice beds with full stomachs. It was pleasant and peaceful, which was good preparation for the challenges that lay ahead on their journey.

After a few days of detour to visit some mission works with local tribes and to minister with Phil Baer, who had helped him in Tuxtla Gutierrez all those years ago, Nate and Henry flew out of Ixtapa. They moved on across Guatemala, Honduras, Panama, and Colombia. They faced engine troubles, inaccurate maps, inadequate food and accommodations, and violent illnesses. Finally, God guided them across the border into Ecuador. Following a brief stop in Quito, they headed for Shell Mera. Nate was grateful to be home, back where he felt he truly belonged.

Despite Nate's challenges during his trip, he had still fared better than Marj. She and the children had not been fortunate at all in their travels. They flew from Los Angeles, California to Mexico City just after Nate and Henry left. That flight was uneventful, but in Mexico City, Marj was told the family could not continue their travels.

"But we have tickets," Marj demanded. "Why can't we continue home to Ecuador?"

"You do not have the proper travel visas for your children," the immigration official told her.

Marj looked down at four-year-old Kathy and two-year-old Steve, who were waiting patiently beside her. "The Ecuadorian officials in California assured me my children were too young to require visas," she insisted.

"I'm sorry, ma'am," the official said sternly. "Rules are rules. And our rules say they must have travel visas."

"So what do I do now?" Marj asked, frustration seeping into her voice.

"I cannot help you anymore, ma'am," the immigration official said, waving her to the side. "Next, please!"

Marj sat on a bench with her children while she collected her thoughts. Then she found a phone and started making calls. She visited government officials, pleading and explaining her case. She argued, discussed, and persuaded. Above all, she prayed. And through divine intervention, the Mexican government finally allowed her and the children to continue on to Ecuador.

Marj sent a message to Nate with the joyful news. They had lost some time, but they were finally coming home. When Marj, Kathy, and Steve finally made it to Ecuador, they contacted Nate. He met them in a coastal city. It was a thrilling and thankful reunion, and before long they returned to Shell Mera. They were all together again, and they launched back into the missionary aviation ministry. Little did they know the exciting times that lay ahead in God's plan!

Adventures in Auca Territory

The next few years were a flurry of activity at Shell Mera. When Nate and Marj had first arrived in Ecuador in 1948, there were twelve missionaries being serviced by MAF flights. By the end of 1954, there were more than two dozen missionaries on nine stations that were scattered haphazardly across hundreds of miles of jungle. MAF headquarters finally realized the work was too much for Nate and Marj to handle alone. In the spring of 1955, MAF sent Johnny Keenan and his wife, Ruth, to help at Shell Mera. The Keenans and the Saints immediately became good friends.

Nate was also developing strong friendships with some of the newer missionaries who had come to the jungle. Jim and Betty Elliot, Ed and Marilou McCully, and Pete and Olive Fleming were all sent out by the same missions group. They were young and bright and—like Nate—longed to spread the gospel to tribes that had never seen a Bible or heard God's message of love and forgiveness. Another young missionary couple that shared this vision was Roger and Barbara Youderian. Nate, Jim, Ed, Pete, and Roger were constantly getting together to dream and scheme about new ways to change the world with God's Word.

When Nate wasn't collaborating with his fellow missionaries, he was staying busy with flying and working at home. A Bible institute and hospital had been established at Shell Mera when the Shell Oil Company pulled out of that region of Ecuador. The house needed to be continually expanded, as well, to accommodate the increase in travelers and visitors. In addition, a new member was added to the Saint family during this busy time. In December 1954, Philip Saint was born. Poor Nate and Marj barely had time to think!

One day, Nate was on a routine supply flight to an Ecuadorian Army base at Villano. The airstrip was good, so Nate landed easily and unloaded the requested supplies. As he climbed back into the plane to take off, he heard a shout. Soldiers from the base were asking Nate to wait. They said a local Quichua village needed help. As they spoke, a Quichua Indian emerged from the jungle, panting and waving his arms.

"Please wait," he called to Nate in broken Spanish. "There is a couple from my village. They have been speared by Aucas. Please help them!"

A shiver went down Nate's spine at the thought of a nearby Auca attack. "When did it happen?" he asked.

"Just now," the Quichua answered. "Please, it is a man and his wife. And the wife is about to have a baby."

As the Quichua spoke, several villagers emerged from the jungle carrying the injured woman. She had been speared in the armpit and lower back. The man was still able to walk, and he limped along behind with two spear wounds in his chest, one in his thigh, and a hole straight through his hand. Nate quickly assessed the situation and radioed Marj.

"Shell Mera, this is 56 Henry," he called, giving his call sign.

"Okay, I read you," Marj answered. "What is it?"

"I'm getting ready to head out of Villano, and I have two injured Indians with me. Have a couple of beds ready and a doctor and nurse standing by. They both have spear wounds."

When Nate was done relaying information, he directed the Indians and soldiers to carefully load the injured couple into the airplane. Back at Shell Mera—and later, in Quito—the Quichuas were treated and eventually recovered. But seeing those gaping spear wounds reopened an old hole in Nate's heart. The Auca people had made those wounds. They needed Jesus, and Nate knew God wanted to use him to reach them.

Nate's sister, Rachel, was finally settled into the Ecuadorian mission station at Hacienda Ila, not too far from Shell Mera. In a letter, she told Nate there was a young woman named Dayuma at the hacienda. When she was just a teenager, Dayuma had fled her Auca tribe because they threatened to spear her. Rachel was working with Dayuma to learn the Auca dialect so the Bible could be translated into words and expressions the Auca people would understand. When Nate heard this news, his heart soared. It seemed God was opening doors faster than Nate ever dreamed.

Although none of the missionaries had ever seen an actual Auca settlement, they knew from other tribes which parts of the jungle were considered Auca territory. In the late spring of 1955, Ed McCully and his wife, Marilou, decided to move to Arajuno, an abandoned oil depot just inside Auca territory. They would use the base to minister to the local Quichua Indians, and they hoped someday it might be the base for operations to the Aucas as well.

The move was considered risky by the surrounding tribes, and many tried to dissuade Ed from the move. He was encroaching on Auca land, and the Aucas had killed for much less. But Nate and Ed worked hard to fix up the station, and Ed moved his family into their new home without incident. They were closer than any outsider had been to the Aucas in decades. The missionaries silently hoped Ed's move to Arajuno would be the first small step on the road to reaching the Auca people.

On September 19, 1955, Nate made his usual supply run to Arajuno. Ed and Marilou greeted him with cookies and joyful expressions. After a time of fellowship and shared laughter, Nate turned to Ed.

"Want to go up on a little airborne hunt with me?" Nate asked.

"Sure," Ed said, gulping down the last cookie. "What are we hunting?"

"Auca settlements," Nate replied.

Marilou cleared the empty cookie plate. "Well, you boys have fun. And please, try to have him home by dinner time."

Nate grinned and saluted. "Yes, ma'am!"

The two men scrambled like schoolboys into the cockpit of the bright yellow plane. Nate had some extra fuel and a few extra hours of daylight. The air was clear and the sky was cloudless. It was a rare opportunity, and the men were eager to seize it. After they had flown for several minutes, Nate turned to Ed.

"Do you see anything?" he asked.

"Nothing," Ed said sadly. "Not a break in the trees. Not a clearing. Not a wisp of smoke from a campfire. Nothing."

Nate eyed the fuel gauge carefully. "Well, we've got a bit of fuel left. Let's fly around a little more. Keep your eyes peeled."

Nate and Ed stared out the windshield until their eyes hurt. Nate checked the gauges frequently. Finally, he knew they had to turn back.

"I'm sorry, Ed," Nate said. "We're getting too low on fuel. Maybe next time we can—wait! What's that?"

Nate pointed to a tiny break in the trees. Ed strained to see it, and Nate adjusted his course and flew right toward the little spot of brown in the canopy of green. As they got nearer, the spot became a clearing. Then it became an entire little village of thatched roofs.

"There they are!" Ed whooped. "There they are!"

"Praise God!" Nate hollered.

It seemed like they had accomplished the impossible. God had led them over miles of endless jungle to one tiny settlement, but they felt like they had just discovered a new world. They had finally found the elusive Aucas!

Operation Auca is Imagined

Ten days after the first sighting, on September 29, Nate was on a flight with Pete Fleming when he spotted another, larger settlement. This one was only fifteen minutes by air from Ed's home at Arajuno. God was opening doors for contact with the Auca tribe, and Nate felt God's guiding hand urging him forward. He contacted his friends, Jim Elliot and Roger Youderian. Jim and Roger agreed to meet Nate, Pete, and Ed at Shell Mera to discuss a potential outreach to the Aucas.

Within days, the five missionary men and Nate's co-worker at Shell Mera, Johnny Keenan, were huddled around a map on the floor of Nate's living room.

"So we have seen a settlement here and here," Nate said, jabbing the map in two places with bright red circles around them. "That's all the settlements we have seen so far, but there must be more."

"Well, for now, let's focus on the settlements we know about," Ed said. "What do you propose we do to make first contact?"

"We could drop gifts," Roger suggested. "That might make them think more favorably of us."

"I like that idea," said Nate, scribbling something on a notepad. "Any idea what kind of gifts they would like? I mean, we wouldn't want them to think we're dropping off our castoffs and leftovers."

"The Quichuas like shiny things," Ed advised. "Maybe something like an aluminum kettle or some ribbons or buttons. They like tools, too. There is nothing more valuable to the Indians than a machete. And I imagine the Aucas are not so different from the Quichuas."

Nate was taking notes furiously as Ed spoke. "Good, good," he murmured.

"I think we should learn some basic phrases from that Dayuma girl at Hacienda Ila," said Jim, who had visited the hacienda recently. "And then I say we go in on foot and talk to them face-to-face."

"That sounds unnecessarily dangerous," Pete said, shifting in his chair. "I think we should do more research. We should learn more about these people. We should learn their language. We should become familiar with their culture. Then we can make contact."

"There has to be balance," Nate said. "Jim, I understand your eagerness, but Pete has a point. We can't plunge into this situation without thorough preparation. We must be good stewards of our resources and our lives, and if we get speared on the first day, how can we reach them with the gospel?"

The men sipped hot cocoa as they discussed and debated. They prayed and plotted and planned as the meeting went into the wee hours of the morning. And on that night, on the floor of Nate's living room at Shell Mera, a plan called Operation Auca was born.

It was decided that, for the time being, Operation Auca would be kept secret. Only the five men involved, their families, and Johnny and Ruth Keenan knew about the plan. They did not want outsiders potentially interfering with what they felt was God's plan for reaching the Auca people. They did not need nosy anthropologists and slick journalists compromising contact that had been decades in the making. It was important to keep the first several phases of the plan completely under wraps.

The first step of the journey would involve flyovers and gift drops. In this phase, the missionaries also hoped to make voice contact with a speaker system on the plane. The later phases of the plan involved finding a suitable landing strip near the village, making face-to-face contact, and eventually establishing a mission outpost. Each missionary was given a job and set of responsibilities. With the plan in place, the missionaries got right to work.

Since Jim Elliot had been introduced to Dayuma at Hacienda Ila and she was familiar with him, it was decided that Jim would work on learning simple phrases in the Auca language. He was a born linguist, and he spent several days at Hacienda Ila with Dayuma and a stack of note cards. She taught him a phrase, and he wrote it phonetically on a card, along with the meaning. Then Jim repeated the phrases back to Dayuma, and she corrected his pronunciation until he got it right. The Indian languages were very complex, and the Auca language was no exception. It was a long, tedious process, and it only resulted in Jim learning a few very basic phrases, but it was a start.

In the meantime, Nate was working on an automatic release for his bucket-drop system. In its current form, the system required the recipient to come and take items from the bucket while it dangled from the plane. But Nate felt it was unreasonable to expect the wary Aucas to eagerly approach a gift that was dangling from a plane. If he could automatically release the gift, however, he trusted the curiosity of the tribe would prompt them to come find the gift when the plane was gone. He tested several systems on the airstrip at Shell Mera with Johnny Keenan's help.

"Did it work?" Nate asked when he had landed after a particularly promising test. "Did the bucket detach and stay?"

Johnny shook his head. "You're close, but it isn't detaching. It's getting hung up on the line. Maybe it just can't be done."

Nate grinned. "Is that a challenge? Trust me. I'm going to figure this out."

After several more tries, Nate finally succeeded by cutting up one of Marj's old brooms. He attached the broom handle to the drop line and through the connector that held the gift on the line. When the broom handle hit the ground, it created slack on the line and the dropped item was effectively released. Then the line could be safely retracted into the plane, leaving the gift behind.

The auto-release system was ready. The basic phrases in the Auca language were learned. The first gift was all set up. It was a shiny aluminum kettle tied with bright, flowing ribbons and filled with assorted buttons and a small packet of rock salt. All of the pieces were in place. All of the players were ready. After plenty of prayers and a few sleepless nights, Nate and Ed McCully took off on an early October morning. They were headed for the Auca village. It was time to make first contact. Operation Auca was a go!

Operation Auca is Implemented

The small yellow plane circled lazily two thousand feet over the path to the Auca village. The aluminum kettle dangled far below, ribbons dancing in the breeze. With a gentle thud, the gift touched the ground and was released from the line. The first attempt at contact had been made.

"I wish we had seen at least one Auca," Ed commented as they turned toward home.

"Maybe they are afraid of the airplane," Nate said. "They could be hiding in their homes when they hear the engines. In this noisy bird, we can't really sneak up on them."

"I guess," Ed said. "But what if the village is deserted? Or what if they don't use that trail anymore? They'll never find our gift."

Nate squinted toward the sunny horizon. "All we can do is pray and wait," he said. "That's what we have to do, Ed: pray and wait."

When Nate and Ed flew over the Auca village a week later, they got their answer. The kettle was gone. But there were still no Aucas in sight. They began to circle in the sky, first in large circles, then tighter and tighter. They let down their second gift. It was a machete, one of the most highly-prized tools of the jungle. Suddenly, Ed let out an ear-splitting whoop.

"Nate, I see one!" he shouted, scrambling to the open cargo door with his binoculars in hand. "I see an Auca!"

Nate grinned. "Well, don't fall out of the plane, brother! We don't want to offer you as a gift. Not yet, anyway. Now, tell me what you see."

Ed peered through the binoculars. "There is an Auca man who just came from the house into the clearing. He is looking up at the plane."

Ed lowered the machete further as the plane settled into a tight circle. "Hey! Now there are two more men in the clearing," Ed hollered. "Nate! There are three of them! They are all watching the machete go down."

"Is it almost on the ground?" Nate asked.

"Almost," Ed answered. "But I'm afraid it's going to hit the house. Wait . . . wait . . . nope. It's not going to hit the house. But it is going in the water."

"Can you change the direction?" Nate wondered.

"Not at this point," Ed said. "It just splashed down, and—Nate! The first Auca man just dived in after it!"

The Auca waded into the water, retrieved the machete, and brought it back to shore. Within minutes, several more Auca men crowded around the first man. They examined the machete with great interest, frequently glancing up at the airplane. Nate and Ed were ecstatic!

By the next gift drop, one week later, the release mechanism was no longer necessary. The Aucas were waiting when they heard the plane. They eagerly approached the bucket when it was lowered. The missionaries dropped clothing, tools, and other small items each week. And the Aucas were increasingly unafraid, waving at the plane and openly celebrating its arrival and the gifts it brought. Nate and Ed tried using a loudspeaker to call out some of the Auca phrases Jim had taught the team. They said, "We like you!" over and over, hoping it made them seem more friendly.

When the gift was removed on the sixth drop, Ed felt a pull on the line.

"Nate, they don't seem to want me to bring up the bucket yet," Ed commented. "What do you think?"

"Leave it down there for a few minutes," Nate said. "Let's see what happens."

Nate continued to fly in tight circles, and when the line went slack again, Ed pulled it up. When he pulled it into the plane, he was flabbergasted. Inside was a beautiful feathered crown! The Aucas had sent a return gift.

From that day on, each drop involved an exchange of gifts. The missionaries dropped tools and other items. In return, the Aucas offered up trinkets and valuables from their culture. Although they still faced cultural and linguistic barriers, the Aucas and the missionaries were communicating in their own way.

God was bringing them closer to making face-to-face contact.

Soon, the missionaries began to see clear signs that their flights were welcomed by the villagers. The Aucas cleared away some of the taller trees surrounding their homes. They also built an air traffic control platform of sorts to be nearer to the plane. On one visit, Nate and Ed were surprised to see a model airplane, remarkably similar to Nate's MAF plane, attached to the thatched roof of one of the houses. A relationship was developing daily between the missionaries in the yellow plane above and the Aucas in the primitive village below.

The Operation Auca team met frequently at Shell Mera to discuss strategies and plans. They each had a different perspective on what their next move should be.

"We should go in on foot, clear an airstrip, and make face-to-face contact," Jim Elliot insisted.

"I don't think the time is right," Pete Fleming argued.

"How could the time not be right?" Jim wondered. "We have established goodwill, and they seem genuinely happy to see us. What better time than the present?"

"I just think we should learn more about their language and culture before we go traipsing in there," Pete countered. "Meet with Dayuma more. Learn more about the intricacies of Auca life. Then we will be better equipped to minister to them effectively."

"I see your point, Pete," Ed said, "but I also share Jim's enthusiasm. This is a good time. I say we look for an area that would be easy to clear for an airstrip, maybe something a few miles from the village. When God provides an airstrip location, I say we go in."

"Exactly," Jim said. "We can't waste the strides we have made by waiting. It could take years to understand the culture."

Nate smiled at the passionate men in the room. "You all have good ideas," he said. "But let's not get ahead of ourselves. You all know I tend to be a cautious fellow. I'm not opposed to looking for potential airstrip locations, but at the same time, I don't want to get ahead of God."

"Agreed," said Roger Youderian. "So what's the plan?"

"Well," Nate said, "if it's up to me, I say we continue the drops as usual. As we fly to and from the village, we will look for nearby airstrip locations. And Jim, see if you can pick up more information from Dayuma. I don't want to rush into anything, but when the time is right, I don't want to be even a little bit unprepared."

The members of the Operation Auca team agreed that Nate's plan was sound and reasonable. Nate and Ed would continue the weekly gift drops. Jim would learn more about the culture from Dayuma and teach what he learned to the team. Pete and Roger would continue to pray for the mission and the Auca people. They all trusted that God would show them the right time to make face-to-face contact.

The gift drops continued for thirteen weeks. One week, Nate and Ed dropped a live chicken, carefully secured in the bucket. The next week, the Aucas' return gift was a live parrot in a cage. Nate gave the parrot to his son, Steve, who was nearly five years old. Steve loved the gift and prayed for the Aucas who had given him his new pet.

As he made the drops, Nate always kept his eyes open for usable land that would be easy to clear. He also looked for a possible ready-made landing area along the nearby Curaray River. He figured a long, smooth patch of beach would be his best option for landing the plane. He wasn't in a hurry, but he knew that someday the Operation Auca ministry would move from gift exchanges to personal contact, and he wanted to be ready whenever God opened that door. It didn't take long before Nate saw the door swing gloriously open.

The Next Step

On December 10th, gifts were exchanged as usual. As he flew away from the village, however, Nate noticed something he had never seen before.

"Look down there, Ed," Nate said, banking the plane slightly. "Look at the Curaray. Notice anything?"

Ed looked down. "I've never seen that beach before," he said. "Where did that come from?"

"The river does tend to change with the seasons," Nate said. "It looks like a sandbar. But it's pretty wide and pretty long. And it seems flat."

Ed grinned at Nate. "Are you thinking what I'm thinking?"

"Of course," Nate said, grinning back at him. "Looks like a perfect landing strip from up here. It's only four or five miles from the village, and it looks like there are trails directly to this part of the river. Shall we go lower and have a better look around?"

"You bet," Ed said.

Nate circled around and took a second pass over the sandbar, much lower and slower. The sandbar arched up out of the river near a wooded bank. It looked good from above, but much remained unknown. Was it long enough to land the Piper Cruiser aircraft Nate was flying? Was it solid enough, or would they sink in and get stuck? Nate had to find out. He flew high again and turned again for another pass.

"In the back of the plane are several paper sacks," Nate told Ed. "Get them and wait by the cargo door. When I tell you to drop one, drop it right away."

"I can do that," Ed said. "But what are we doing?"

"Measuring the airstrip," Nate said. "I have a system I use with perfectly-timed drops of bags of colored paint powder."

Ed laughed. "Sounds like a typical Nate Saint method," he said, crawling into the back of the plane to retrieve the bags.

With the bags in hand, Ed waited by the open cargo door. Nate came around toward the sandbar. He slowed his airspeed and dipped lower than before. As they approached the beginning of the sandbar, Nate shouted to Ed. Ed dropped a bag. It exploded in a burst of color that marked the beginning of the makeshift runway. Nate counted out loud and, as they neared the end of the runway, shouted to Ed again. Ed dropped another bag. Nate pulled the plane up and away from the river, carefully surveying the paint powder marks.

"It's definitely long enough," Nate commented. "Not by too much, but it does still give us a little bit of wiggle room."

"So, we're good then?" Ed asked.

"Not quite," Nate said. "There's one more thing to check."

He circled the plane and came in for one more pass. This time, he got lower and lower and lower. Ed was gripping his seat. Finally, the wheels of the plane touched the sandbar. Nate felt a slight give beneath the wheels, but the ground held. He pulled the plane up and off the sandbar. It was firm enough and long enough. They had their landing strip, and they hadn't even had to hike in and clear it by hand.

God had just opened a new door for the Operation Auca team. With a renewed sense of joy and excitement, Nate and Ed flew to Shell Mera and contacted the other members of the team. Within days, the team was again assembled in Nate's living room. Plans for a new phase of ministry were discussed.

"The rains will be coming soon," Nate said. "We're more than halfway through December, and by late January the rains will come. That sandbar won't make it through the rainy season."

"And without a landing strip, our job is that much harder," Ed added. "We'd have to make one ourselves. And we all know how hard that can be."

"We need to take advantage of this open door," Roger agreed.

"So let's go soon," Jim proposed, his voice brimming with excitement. "We could go tomorrow, as far as I'm concerned."

"But it's almost Christmas," Pete argued. "Let's spend Christmas with our families. Then we can go."

"Pete's right," Nate said. "Let's be with our families for Christmas. We can go just after the new year begins. How does that sound?"

They all agreed, and the plans were set. They would fly in at the next full moon, January 3, 1956. They dubbed the new airstrip "Palm Beach" after the palms that lined the banks of the Curaray River. They also drew up plans for a prefabricated tree house to provide safety and shelter during their time at Palm Beach. The tree house would be built at Shell Mera. Then it would be broken into large parts to be flown to Palm Beach, where it would be reassembled.

The team also discussed what they would do when they met the Aucas. What if they were unfriendly? Other outsiders had commented that the Aucas seemed to be afraid of guns, which they called "fire sticks." The members of the Operation Auca team were divided on whether to carry and use guns or leave them behind. They finally decided to carry guns as a deterrent, but not to use them on the Aucas under any circumstances.

All five men agreed that if given the choice between killing an Auca and dying themselves, they would choose to die. After all, the team members knew they would go to heaven because they had trusted in Jesus as Savior, but the Aucas had never even heard of Jesus and had no existing hope of salvation. This unanimous, selfless decision was an eerie premonition of what God had in store for Operation Auca.

First Contact

On Tuesday, January 3, 1956, the rising sun found five men preparing for the most thrilling adventure of their lives. The airstrip at Arajuno—the closest airstrip to Palm Beach—was piled high with organized stacks of food, supplies, clothing, utensils and tools, and medical supplies. There were also piles of potential gifts for the Auca village and several radios for contacting the base at Shell Mera. The final mound contained tree house parts to be assembled at Palm Beach. Everything was ready to go.

At 8:02 am, just two minutes behind the set schedule, Nate and Ed climbed into the cockpit of the little plane. They looked at each other and grinned as Nate started the engines. Soon they were airborne.

"It's hard to believe the time has really come," Nate said. "I've been praying about this for so many years. And now God has opened the door. It's unbelievable."

"Do you think we'll meet an Auca today?" Ed wondered.

"I don't know," Nate said. "They seem curious, so they might come right away. Or they might be afraid, so it may take a few days. Either way, we'll be ready."

"I wonder what our ministry with them will be," Ed said. "Do you think they'll be open to hearing the gospel? And how will we communicate with them when we only know a few phrases?"

"I don't know that either," Nate answered. "But it sure seems like this is God's perfect timing, and I want to be in on it. I'm ready to do whatever God wants me to do to reach these people for Christ."

On that first trip to Palm Beach, Nate took only Ed and supplies on board. He wanted a light load for the first real landing on the sandbar. As they neared the beach, the thick fog that had plagued them all morning began to thin out and dissolve to clear skies. Fifteen minutes into the journey, they dropped through the remaining patchy fog and made an initial pass over the makeshift runway to check for obstacles. It was clear, so Nate took the plane back up into the sky, circled, and came in a second time, ready to land.

The sand was soft, but it held up well under the little plane. With excited shouts, Nate and Ed climbed out and unloaded the first batch of supplies. Nate left Ed behind on the beach and went back for Jim and Roger and more supplies. After five flights of personnel and supplies, everything was finally at Palm Beach. The men worked quickly to assemble the tree house high in an ironwood tree. Night was falling quickly, and they needed to be ready for the potential dangers darkness could bring.

"Seems pretty secure," Nate said as he descended from the tree house. "Is there anything else you all need before we take off?"

Jim, Roger, and Ed looked at one another and shook their heads. Nate and Pete said goodbye and climbed into the plane. Because sudden rain could obliterate the sandbar, stranding the plane, it was agreed that Nate and Pete would leave each night, spend the night at Arajuno, and return each morning to spend the day. This schedule soon became routine as the men waited for God to work at Palm Beach.

The days on Palm Beach were full of waiting. The men read books and magazines, talked, napped, and lounged aimlessly on the beach. Every so often, they waded into the shallow Curaray River and immersed themselves as much as possible to escape the pesky mosquitoes. The days seemed to drag on endlessly, and the missionaries wondered if they had misinterpreted God's will. On Friday, they got their answer.

At 11:15 am on Friday, January 6, three Aucas walked onto the narrow shore across the river from Palm Beach. They eyed the missionaries with a mix of suspicion and curiosity.

"Nate ... Nate ..." Ed whispered, nudging his napping friend. "Look across the river."

"What is it?" Nate asked sleepily, his hat over his eyes.

"Aucas! Three of them. Just across the river and watching all of us," Ed answered. "Look, will you?"

Nate opened his eyes and looked. Then he sat up abruptly. The others were instantly alert as well. Outgoing as usual, Jim was the first one on his feet. He plunged into the river and waded across, repeating the phrases Dayuma had taught him.

"We like you," he said in his best version of Auca dialect, motioning for them to cross the river. "We want to meet you. We like you."

The Aucas looked confused. Jim motioned first to the young man, then to the teenage girl and older woman who were with him. He moved slowly back toward the camp at Palm Beach, motioning for the Aucas to follow him. He also kept repeating all of the Auca phrases he could remember. Hesitantly, the Aucas stepped into the water and waded across.

Once on the Palm Beach side of the river, the Aucas explored the camp. They examined the tree house, the firepit, and the men themselves. They seemed friendly, and even though the missionaries could not communicate with them, the contact seemed like a giant leap forward.

"What do we do now that they're here?" asked Pete, a little nervously.

"I don't know," said Roger as he watched the Aucas wander around. "It's impossible to know what they might want."

"I think they want to check everything out thoroughly," said Nate, laughing as the older woman examined his sandy blond hair. "But you're right. It's impossible to tell anything for sure."

"Well, I say we treat them like we would any house guest," said Jim. "And what does that mean?"

Nate grinned. "It means we feed them dinner."

The missionaries cooked up a feast of hamburgers and lemonade. They served the Aucas, who were hesitant to eat until the young man finally tasted a tiny bite. That was all it took. Their guests devoured the food while squatting by the fire. They gulped down the lemonade and chattered and laughed among themselves. The missionaries looked on with joy. Things were going better than they could have ever expected!

"I don't know why," Jim said, "but they don't seem to understand any of the phrases Dayuma taught me."

"Maybe the language has changed," Pete offered. "After all, Dayuma has been gone from the tribe for a while."

"Or maybe Jim just doesn't have very good pronunciation," Nate said with a grin. "But things seem to be going alright without them understanding us fully. And that fellow sure seems interested in the airplane. I wish we knew their names. I hate calling him 'that fellow'."

"Then don't," said Jim. "Let's call him George."

"Why George?" Roger asked.

"I don't know," Jim said. "But why not?"

"George it is," Nate said.

When he finished his food, George approached the airplane out on the sandbar. He looked at Nate and waved at the airplane. Then he pointed to himself and then the sky. He repeated the actions until Nate figured out that George wanted a ride. Nate shrugged and nodded. It might be a way to get through to the whole tribe. If they could see one of their own flying through the sky in the plane, they might see that the missionaries posed no danger to them.

George climbed eagerly into the plane, and Nate started the engines. He zoomed off the beach and banked the plane to fly low over the Auca village. George was ecstatic! He scrambled to the door of the plane and tried to climb out on the wing. Nate stretched out his arm and snatched George, pulling him back inside. Thankfully, George got the idea. He stayed at the open door, however, nearly falling out as he waved to his friends far below. In the village, Aucas ran shouting and pointing up at George. He grinned and shouted back.

Nate finally turned back and landed at the camp. Evening was settling in. He and Pete needed to leave for Arajuno, but they were reluctant to end such a glorious day. As they prepared to leave, George and the teenage girl crossed the river and disappeared into the jungle. The older woman yelled after them, but they did not return. The old woman shook her head sadly. Then she curled up by the fire and went to sleep.

"Do we just leave her there?" Ed wondered.

"Why not?" said Jim. "If she's still there in the morning, we'll feed her again."

Nate smiled. "Jim, you've got food on the brain," he teased. "Listen, I don't think she poses a threat. But this gathering darkness poses a threat to us. Pete and I have to get out of here."

"We'll see you tomorrow," Roger said. "Who knows what will happen next?"

After saying final goodbyes, Nate and Pete flew out toward Arajuno. Roger, Ed, and Jim climbed up into their tree house. They took one last look at the Auca woman sleeping by the fire below. They were all astounded by the amazing events of the day. It left them wondering what God would do next.

Last Contact

Saturday was a day of waiting again at Palm Beach. The five men lounged around, hoping that George and his friends would return and bring other Aucas to meet them. They prayed for God's guidance, and they prayed for more contact. When it finally became evident nothing new was going to happen, Nate and Pete gathered up the film from Friday's Auca encounter. Then they said goodnight to their friends and took off for Arajuno.

Sunday morning, January 8th, Nate radioed Marj.

"So, honey, how are things at good old Shell Mera?" Nate asked.

"Oh, nothing new. We just sit around all day and wait for news from you," Marj teased. "Remember, you're the one with the exciting life."

Nate laughed. "Now, I know better than that. You're coordinating all of Johnny's mission flights in between keeping tabs on me. Not to mention three little tykes swarming around your feet. Come to think of it, you don't sound busy at all."

"Exactly," said Marj. "It's just the same old routine around here. I think I'll send the children to Sunday School with Olive this morning. That way I can stay by the radio in case you need to reach me. Are you leaving Arajuno soon?"

"I have a few things to do first," Nate said. "I want to develop this film from Friday's visit."

"I can't wait to see those pictures," Marj said. "Was there any more contact yesterday?"

"Nothing," Nate answered, his voice laced with frustration. "But we need your prayers today."

"I'm always praying for you all," Marj assured him.

"Well, I know that, honey," Nate said. "But I have a feeling about today. Today is the day things will happen."

Marj knew Nate's feelings were often right in tune with God's will. "In that case, I promise to redouble my prayer efforts," she told him.

"Thanks. I can always count on you," Nate said with a smile. "I guess I better get going. I'll radio again at 12:30."

"Roger that," Marj said. "I'll be praying for you. Talk to you at 12:30."

Marj stayed by the radio that morning, praying and monitoring the airwaves. Olive Fleming, Pete's wife, was also staying at Shell Mera. Marj caught her in the hallway and relayed Nate's news, as well as the request for prayer. Both wives bowed their heads and prayed right there in the hall. They wanted every minute of Operation Auca to be under God's control.

At Marj's request, Olive got all the children together and hurried them off to Sunday School.

The two wives tried to keep everything as normal as possible, but there was an undercurrent of excitement in the air. Nate thought something big was going to happen. They knew it could be the day they had all waited and prayed to see!

When Nate's voice crackled in over the airwaves at 12:30, it was brimming with excitement.

"Shell Mera, come in. Come in, Shell Mera," he called out.

"This is Shell Mera," Marj answered. "What is it?"

"I'm in the air and on my way to Palm Beach with Pete," Nate said. "We just flew past the village, and it seemed empty and quiet. That's pretty unusual for a Sunday afternoon."

"What do you think it means?" Marj asked.

"Well, Pete and I were wondering the same thing as we flew toward the beach," Nate answered. "And then, just now, we looked down and saw a group of nearly a dozen Aucas heading along the trail that connects the village to the beach. They're coming, Marj!"

"Oh, Nate! That's wonderful," Marj said.

"You bet it is! At this rate, they should be at the beach in time for an afternoon worship service," Nate observed. "What a blessed Sunday! Keep those prayers coming, honey. It looks like we're going to need them today."

"We'll be praying," Marj promised. "What time should I expect your next check in?"

Nate did some quick time calculations in his head. "Let's say 4:30," he told her. "That should give us plenty of time to get acquainted."

"I'll be waiting," Marj said. "Talk to you at 4:30."

What Nate and his friends did not know was that George and the teenage girl who had visited the camp had returned to the village full of lies about the missionaries. They told the villagers that the missionaries tried to harm them, poison them, and hold them captive. Although the older woman refuted these stories, the villagers believed the lies. They decided the only way to avoid being attacked by the missionaries was to attack first. That was why they were hurrying through the jungle on that fateful Sunday afternoon.

When Nate landed at Palm Beach, he and Pete could barely contain their excitement.

"They're coming, fellows," Nate said, leaping from the plane, "a whole gang of them! It looked like nearly a dozen or more."

"And they're coming fast," Pete said, catching the excitement. "I'd say they'll be here in an hour or two."

"Praise God!" Ed said.

Jim clapped his hands. "Today's the day!" he shouted. "Praise God, today's the day!"

The team members were thrilled. This was exactly what they had hoped for. They took a few minutes to pray together, thanking God and asking for wisdom and guidance. Then they planned a meal to serve to their guests. They practiced their few Auca phrases over and over, correcting each other's pronunciation. Then they waited eagerly, unable to stop smiling.

When the warriors attacked, it was sudden and swift. They snuck soundlessly into the camp and announced their presence with soaring spears. Joy turned to confusion and panic as the surprised missionaries faced their attackers. They fired a few warning shots into the air as they had agreed to do, but they did not run or actively defend themselves. They faced their deaths as they had lived their lives: with the calm assurance they were in the center of God's will.

Fueled by their passionate anger and fear, the Auca attackers slaughtered all five men with rapid brutality. When the missionaries were dead, the Auca warriors threw their belongings into the Curaray River, where several of the bodies rested. With victorious shouts, they invaded the sandbar and climbed up on the little plane parked there. They viciously tore into the fabric fuselage, pulling the yellow cloth from the plane in long strips. Soon streamers were all that remained of the sturdy covering.

When they had done all the damage they could do, the Aucas headed back down the narrow trail to their village. Palm Beach was strewn with bodies and boxes of supplies and golden shreds of fabric. The air was still and silent. 4:30 came and went, and Nate missed his call in. His watch was stopped at 3:12 pm, the moment when it was smashed on a rock as Nate's lifeless, spear-riddled body fell into the Curaray River.

The Aftermath

When Nate missed his 4:30 call in, Marj felt a tiny twinge of worry. It was unlike Nate to miss a call in, but Marj knew that in the damp jungle climate, radio equipment malfunctioned regularly. She went into the living room where Olive was sitting.

"Nate missed his 4:30 call in," she announced.

Olive looked up and studied Marj's face. "Are you concerned?"

"Not really," Marj said. "But maybe a little bit."

"Well," Olive reasoned, "they could just be having a great meeting with all those Aucas. Maybe he just lost track of time or forgot."

"Maybe," Marj said. "It just doesn't seem like Nate."

"Want to pray about it?" Olive asked.

Marj nodded, and the two women bowed their heads and brought their husbands before the Lord. Afterward, Marj felt better. She and Olive decided there was nothing to be worried about, and they hurried to prepare dinner for the household. In the flurry of activity, Marj forgot all about her concerns.

When dinner was over, however, and dusk had come and gone, Marj stood in the doorway and stared into the ebony darkness. There had been no call. The twinge of worry grew into a gnawing fear. Marj knew it was unlikely that the radio and the plane had both broken down on the same day. She went to the radio room.

"56 Henry," she called over the airwaves, using Nate's call sign. "56 Henry, come in. 56 Henry, this is Shell Mera. Come in, 56 Henry."

The radio crackled back at her, an empty, staticky sound. She fought a sense of panic and decided to try calling Marilou at Arajuno.

"They haven't shown up here," Marilou said when Marj reached her on the radio. "I was hoping maybe Nate and Pete had flown all the way out to Shell Mera."

"No," Marj said. "We haven't heard from them since just after noon. They missed their 4:30 call in, and now they didn't make it out to your place."

Marilou could hear the edge in Marj's voice. "Do you think something is wrong?" she asked.

Marj hesitated. "I don't know," she admitted, "but it's beginning to feel that way. Just keep praying. That's all we can do until morning."

"If I see them or hear from them, I'll let you know," Marilou offered.

"Perfect. And if I hear anything, I'll radio you," Marj promised.

The two women said goodnight, but Marj stayed by the radio. She kept waiting and hoping for Nate's cheerful voice to break the silence. She wrestled with her rising panic. Then she called Olive in and radioed the other wives. They might as well all be praying for their husbands out there in the jungle.

It was a long, dark night for the five missionary wives. All they could do was pray and cling to hope. No one slept. As the sun came up, Johnny Keenan was already out on the airstrip readying the second MAF plane. He took off with the sunrise and headed straight for the coordinates for Palm Beach that Nate had given him.

As he flew, Johnny prayed out loud. He asked God to let him find the five men, waving happily, bent over a broken radio and a stranded plane. He prayed that things would be fine, and that the meeting with the Aucas had gone so well that Nate and Pete had stayed the night in a spirit of rejoicing. By the time he reached Palm Beach, Johnny almost had himself convinced of a happy ending.

As he flew over the river, he looked down at the narrow sandbar and his heart sank. He radioed Marj.

"I'm here, Johnny," Marj said breathlessly. "Olive is here, too. Are you there yet?"

"I'm right over Palm Beach," Johnny said, with a catch in his voice.

Marj heard the tone of his voice and felt tears push against her eyelids. "Tell me what you see, Johnny," she ordered gently, her voice low and calm.

"I can see the shell of the plane," he said. "All of the fuselage is torn off and strewn all over the beach."

"What else?" Marj asked.

"Well, that's just it," Johnny said. "I see fabric from the plane and supplies and things thrown everywhere, but there are no signs of life. And Marj, there are no bodies."

"What does that mean, Johnny?" Marj asked.

"Well, I would think it means they might still be alive. But I don't know. All I know is they were here. The plane is evidence of that." Johnny sighed. "I'm going to head back in. We need to organize a search party."

As Johnny signed off and headed back toward Shell Mera, Marj knew in her heart that Nate was dead. She was certain, even though Johnny had not seen any bodies. But instead of the expected rush of paralyzing grief, Marj felt a sense of peace flowing through her. She knew Nate had died doing the Lord's work, which was exactly what he wanted. Olive laid a hand on Marj's shoulder, and Marj gave Olive's hand a gentle squeeze. And when she looked up at Olive, Marj saw the same peace in Olive's eyes that she had felt in her heart. Although they did not understand God's plan, they both knew God's will had been done.

With Johnny's discovery, the veil of secrecy was torn from Operation Auca. Military, media, and missionaries descended upon Shell Mera. Both the American and Ecuadorian militaries launched massive search efforts. Photographers from *Time* and *Life* magazines and dozens of other outlets clamored for interviews and pictures. Missionaries from the radio station in Quito, MAF, and around the world came to offer prayers and comfort. And in New York, Sam Saint—then an executive with American Airlines—abandoned a pile of papers on a conference table and flew to Ecuador.

The house at Shell Mera became more of a headquarters than a home during those long days. The wives brought their children and stayed in guest rooms to be closer to the news. Rachel traveled from Hacienda Ila to be with Marj and the children. The living room was a strange hub of press conferences, news releases, strategy meetings, and prayer sessions. There was activity around the clock; no one wanted to rest until they knew the fate of the five fearless followers of Christ.

The waiting seemed endless, and the wives felt helpless as the search parties came and went.

"Do you think they will ever find them?" Marilou wondered.

"Whether they do or don't," Barbara Youderian answered, "we will have to make peace within ourselves."

"That's the strange thing," Marj said. "I have peace. I feel like I know they're gone, but I am at peace with that fact. Does that seem strange?"

"Not at all," Betty said, crossing the room and giving Marj a squeeze. "I feel the same way. I feel like I should be angry or sad or worried, but I just feel a sense of peace with God's will."

"I guess I'm still sad," Olive said. "But I think God has given us peace as part of our testimony before all these people who are here."

"And it's not just these people," Marj reminded them. "The whole world is watching us. We are carrying on our husbands' legacies in everything we do."

That afternoon, Wednesday, January 11th, the first two bodies were spotted from the air. But although there were tears shed for memories that would never be made together, the indescribable calm and peace remained in the hearts of the five wives. And as the days dragged by and the hope of finding anyone alive dwindled, the women knew that God was in control, and their souls rested in that fact.

Days after spotting the first two bodies, a search party sent in to recover them located the bodies of the others as well. In the face of a mounting tropical storm, the five men were hastily buried beneath the ironwood tree at Palm Beach. The wives felt this was a final resting place befitting the men's mission. Torrential rain fell in sheets and the wind whipped the palm fronds violently, drenching the workers who filled in the grave. It was as if the very heavens themselves were mourning such a great loss.

In the darkness and noise of the storm, the weary, burdened search party returned to Shell Mera. As they entered the house, something caught their attention.

"Is that singing?" a tall soldier asked the man next to him.

"I think so," the man answered. "But who would be singing at a time like this?"

The group, along with several others, made their way to the little living room. The wives and children were gathered there. Marilou sat at the piano, playing joyfully, despite the tears that coursed down her cheeks. Beside her, Betty sang out their prayer before the world.

"We rest on Thee, our Shield and our Defender," she sang. "We go not forth alone against the foe. Strong in Thy Strength, safe in Thy keeping tender, we rest on Thee, and in Thy name we go."

All around the sprawling house, heads lifted and hearts opened. Dedicated missionaries fell to their knees and offered a prayer. Battle-weary soldiers removed their hats and bowed their heads. Hardened reporters dropped their pens and wiped tears from their eyes.

The tall soldier shook his head as he removed his hat and swiped at a tear on his cheek. "I've never seen anything like this!" he said.

Even in death, Nate Saint and his companions were being used by God to touch hearts and change lives. Death was not the end of Nate Saint's story or his ministry.

God Meant It for Good

Within weeks, the stirring saga of the Operation Auca team and their faithful families had circled the globe. What Satan had meant as defeat, God meant for good. Everyone wanted to know more about Nate Saint, his friends, the Auca people, and missionary aviation. Around the world, thousands of people came to know Christ, and hundreds surrendered their lives to mission work, all as a direct result of Operation Auca. God was still using Nate Saint to change the world.

One person who caught Nate's vision for the Auca people—later known by their proper name, the name they called themselves, Waodani—was Rachel Saint, Nate's older sister. She became burdened for the needs of the Waodani people, and she continued to work with Dayuma at Hacienda Ila. Rachel learned from Dayuma more about the Waodani culture, and in return, Rachel taught Dayuma about the grace of God. In 1957, the year after the massacre at Palm Beach, Dayuma became the first Waodani Christian.

In November 1957, Betty Elliot—Jim's wife—was still working in the Ecuadorian jungle when she heard of a Waodani woman who had left the tribe in search of Dayuma. Betty found herself often praying for this woman, and for the whole tribe. One day, God brought an opportunity for ministry into Betty's life.

"Hello," a voice said one day as Betty worked in her yard.

Betty looked up, startled to see two tribal women before her. "Hello. Can I help you?"

"We are looking for Dayuma," the younger woman said in broken Spanish. The older lady beside her nodded. "Do you know Dayuma?"

Betty stood and nodded. "I do," she said. "Would you like me to show you where she lives?"

"Yes," said the younger woman. "We would like to see her."

"Wait," the older woman said. "Your husband was killed by our people."

"Yes," Betty said. "He was. Last year."

"I saw him at the beach," the older woman said. "I ate their food and slept by their fire. They were kind men. They should not have been killed."

Betty felt tears welling up in her eyes. She realized this must have been the older woman who visited with George and the younger woman. She had heard the stories. And she knew this was no coincidence. God wanted Betty to see the Waodani people the way He did, as souls that were lost and directionless without a Savior.

With new understanding, Betty took the women to see Dayuma and Rachel. The Waodani women were overjoyed to see Dayuma alive and well after so many years. They stayed for several months, teaching Betty and Rachel more about the modern Waodani language and culture. But the desire to return to Waodani ways became too strong after a while. In the late summer of 1958, the two Waodani women and Dayuma said goodbye to their friends and disappeared into the welcoming jungle.

For a while, it seemed all contact with the Waodani was lost forever. A few weeks later, Marj Saint came to visit Betty. They went for a walk in the large yard.

"Do you think you'll ever see any of them again?" Marj asked.

"I don't know," Betty admitted. "I thought a new door was open, but now it seems to be slammed shut. Sometimes I just can't see God's plan."

"At least we can have faith that He has one," Marj said. "And trusting in that gives some measure of comfort."

"I know," Betty said. "But sometimes I wonder if I'm missing something. I want to do God's work, but I want to do it His way, not mine."

"I'm sure He will show you His plan when the time is right," Marj encouraged.

The two women walked in silence for a few moments. Then Betty stopped and tipped her head to the side.

"Do you hear that, Marj?" she asked.

"Hear what?"

Betty put a finger to her lips. "It sounds like singing," she whispered.

From the edge of the nearby jungle, they could hear the sounds of singing. As the sound grew louder, Marj and Betty realized someone was singing "Jesus Loves Me" with a Waodani accent. It was Dayuma! She emerged from the jungle with her two Waodani friends and seven others.

After warm greetings and introductions to Marj, the Waodani delegation explained the purpose of their visit. They wanted to invite Rachel, Betty, and Betty's four-year-old daughter, Valerie, to come and live in a Waodani village. The Waodani wanted to learn more about God, whom they called "Man-Maker." Rachel and Betty agreed without hesitation. Nearly three years and many prayers later, the original objectives of Operation Auca were finally being accomplished.

Although Betty Elliot was only able to stay with the Waodani for a few years, Rachel Saint lived the rest of her life—until 1994—among the Waodani. She watched their lives and culture be transformed by God's power. In 1961, Rachel witnessed the baptism of the first Waodani believers. She also helped create Waodani versions of several books of the New Testament, called "God's carvings" by the Waodani people.

Rachel's work was built on the foundation of Nate's legacy, but Nate's son, Steve, has also directly carried on his father's work. As a young boy, Steve often visited his Aunt Rachel in Waodani territory, even after Marj and her children moved back to the United

States. During these visits, Steve learned about the Waodani culture, made new friends, and developed a deep love and forgiveness for the Waodani people.

In 1965, when Steve was fourteen years old, he visited his Aunt Rachel in the village where she worked, which was near Palm Beach.

"Steve, would you like to see your father's grave?" Aunt Rachel asked.

Steve hesitated. He had often wanted to see the place where his father had died trying to save the souls of the Waodani, but he also felt afraid. He didn't know whether seeing the grave would make him angry or sad, or whether it would just help him understand. He remembered well standing on the end of the airstrip and waving goodbye to his smiling father as they launched Operation Auca on that sunny January day. It was just days before Steve's fifth birthday when Nate and his friends left on their mission.

"I guess I'd like to see it," Steve said. "If you think it's a good idea."

"I do," Aunt Rachel said. "It might give you some closure. After all, you were just a little boy when it all happened. Let me tell you the story as you see where it happened. Maybe then it will make more sense."

As Steve stood beneath the ironwood tree, hearing the story and seeing the Curaray River and the weather-worn grave, he felt full forgiveness at work in his heart. He knew that, like his father, he had a special mission to accomplish among the Waodani. To demonstrate his submission to God's will, Steve and his older sister, Kathy, were baptized in the Curaray River a few days later. The two men who performed the baptism were Kimo and Dyuwi, Waodani believers who had been in the party that had killed Nate almost a decade earlier. God was demonstrating to Steve and Kathy that Nate's death was not in vain.

In 1995, after Rachel Saint had died from cancer, the Waodani invited Steve to live and minister with them. The visits he had made to their villages over the years had impressed them, and they wanted him to help them find their way as a culture into the modern world. After much prayer and consideration, Steve Saint, his wife, Ginny, and their four children moved to Ecuador in June of 1995. They established a home among the Waodani and lived and taught there for more than a year, further accomplishing the goals of Nate's ministry.

Nate Saint's dedication and dreams far exceeded his tragically short life. His legacy lives on in the heart of every Waodani believer and thousands of others whose lives have been touched by his testimony. In the end, Nate said it best in his radio broadcast from Quito in 1949, "If God didn't hold back His only Son, but gave Him up to pay the price for our failure and sin, then how can we Christians hold back our lives—the lives He really owns?" Nate Saint offered himself as a living sacrifice to God throughout his life and in his death, and God honored that sacrifice with eternal rewards.

From the Author

Matthew 16:25 says, "For whoever desires to save his life will lose it, but whoever loses his life for my sake will find it." This is a perfect picture of the life of Nate Saint; he gave up his life so God could reveal a greater glory in him and through him. I first heard the story of Operation Auca when I was eight years old, and ever since then I have been inspired by Nate's commitment to the cause of Christ. He was determined to carry out God's will for his life in spite of fears, failures, and physical challenges.

For several years of my life, I lived and ministered with my parents who were missionaries on the island of Jamaica. My experiences during those years gave me a passion for sharing the stories of those who make great sacrifices to carry the gospel around the world. As I wrote this book, learning more about Nate Saint's life—seeing his spirit and his struggles—was both enlightening and encouraging to me.

It is my prayer that this book will provide a window into Nate Saint's vision—his desires, dreams, and dedication. I pray his example will convince young people to step out of their comfort zones and wholeheartedly seek God's will for their lives. That is Nate Saint's legacy: changing the world for Christ, one person and one day at a time.

Nate Saint Timeline

1923	Nate Saint born.
1924	Stalin rises to power in Russia.
1930	Nate's first flight, aged 7 with his brother, Sam.
1933	Nate's second flight with his brother, Sam.
1936	Nate made his public profession of faith.
1937	Nate develops bone infection.
1939	World War II begins.
1940	Winston Churchill becomes British Prime Minister.
1941	Nate graduates from Wheaton College. Nate takes first flying lesson. Japan attacks Pearl Harbor, Hawaii.
1942	Nate's induction into the Army Air Corps.
1943	Nate learns he is to be transferred to Indiana.
1945	Atomic bombs dropped on Hiroshima and Nagasaki, Japan by U.S.
1946	Nate discharged from the Army.
1947	Nate accepted for Wheaton College.
1948	Nate and Marj are married and begin work in Eduador. Nate crashes his plane in Quito.
1949	Nate's first child, Kathy, is born. Germany divided into East and West.

1950	Korean War begins.
1951	Nate's second child, Stephen, is born.
1952	The Saint family return home to the U.S.
1953	Nate comes down with pneumonia.
	Nate and Henry fly to Ecuador.
1954	The first nuclear-powered submarine is launched.
	Nate's third child, Phillip, is born.
1955	Nate is joined by Jim Elliot, Ed McCully, Peter Fleming and Roger Youderian.
	Nate spots an Auca village for the first time.
	Operation Auca commences.
1956	The group sets up camp four miles from the Auca territory.
	Nate and the group are killed on "Palm Beach".

Facts on Ecuador

Ecuador lies in Western South America on the equator. It has quite a varied landscape, from the volcanic islands and sparkling turquoise waters of the Galapagos Islands, to snow covered volcanoes in the Andes, and rain forests and tropical rivers in the Ecuadorian Amazon.

The country is divided ethnically as well as regionally. About ten percent of the population is of European descent, about a quarter belong to indigenous cultures, and the rest are of mostly mixed ethnicity. Those of Spanish descent often are engaged in administration and land ownership in Quito and the surrounding Andean uplands; this is also where most of the indigenous people live—many are farmers.

Guayaquil—the country's largest city, major port, and leading commercial center—is a rival to Quito, the capital.

The predominant religion is Roman Catholicism and the currency is the US dollar.

Industries include petroleum, food processing, textiles, and metal work.

Agriculture includes bananas, coffee, cacao, rice, cattle, balsa wood, fish.

Ecuador's main exports include petroleum, bananas, shrimp, coffee, and cacao.

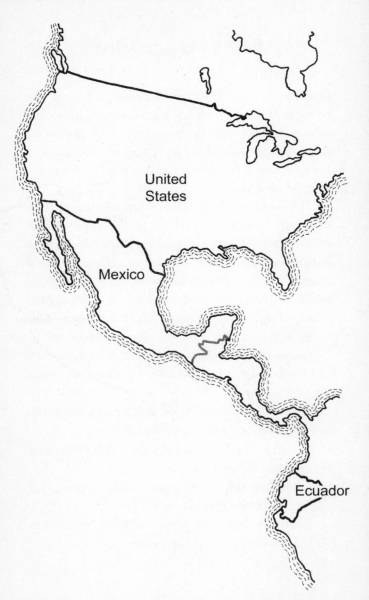

Thinking Further Topics

1. Jeremiah 29:11 says, "For I know the thoughts that I think toward you, saith the Lord, thoughts of peace, and not of evil, to give you an expected end." How do you think God used the early experiences in Nate's life to help shape his future? How did his unconventional upbringing contribute to his abilities as a missionary? How did Nate's experiences in childhood point to the future God had planned for him?

2. Faith is an important component of our lives. What we believe shapes—to a great extent—who we are and how we behave. What role do you think Nate's faith played in his early life? How did faith influence the choices Nate made throughout his life? Do you think his faith played a role in his death? Why or why not?

3. From his first flight at age seven with Sam, Nate was hooked on planes and flying. Pursuing a career related to flying was the dearest desire of Nate's heart. In what ways did Nate's love of flying assist him in serving God? Do you think his love of flying ever kept him from serving God? Explain your answer.

4. Because of a recurrence of the osteomyelitis infection in his leg, Nate was prevented from flying in the Army. He was also kept from serving overseas during World War II. How do you think this disappointment was a part of Nate's plan? How did God use this physical

and emotional challenge to help prepare Nate for ministry? What might have been different in Nate's life if the osteomyelitis had not returned?

5. While Nate was still in the Army, he visited Yosemite National Park with some of his fellow soldiers. While there, he took a hike alone and ended up stranded on a mountain in a snowstorm. What truths about himself and God did Nate discover while on the mountain? Do you think that experience shaped Nate's future decisions and actions? Why or why not?

6. In Proverbs 3:5-6, the Bible says, "Trust in the Lord with all thine heart; and lean not unto thine own understanding. In all thy ways acknowledge Him, and He shall direct thy paths." How do you think Nate's first missionary adventure in Mexico taught him to trust God more? Do you think God was directing Nate's path? In what specific ways did God work in Nate's life while he was in Mexico?

7. After his experiences in Mexico, Nate decided to spend some time in Bible college before continuing with missionary aviation work. Do you think this was a good decision? Do you think Nate would have been more or less effective if he had just jumped right into his aviation ministry? Explain your answer.

8. In Romans 8:28, Paul writes, "And we know that all things work together for good to them that love God, to them who are the called according to his purpose." How do you think Nate's plane crash in Quito worked

for good? What benefits came from that experience? How can you apply the lessons Nate learned in that circumstance to help you through challenges in your own life?

9. God gave Nate a burden to see the salvation of the Auca (Waodani) tribe. Nate wanted to reach these people with the gospel more than anything else in his life. How did this desire motivate Nate? How did it direct and guide his ministry? In what ways did God eventually use Nate to reach the Auca (Waodani) people?

10. Nate's legacy lived on long after his death in a variety of ways. Because of Nate's faithfulness, God is still using his influence to change lives today. What attitudes and actions in Nate's life led to his lasting legacy? How would you describe his legacy? What kind of legacy are you creating through the way you live your life? Does your legacy point others to God?